The Law and The Sabbath

by Allen Walker

Published and Distributed by
Hartland Publications
Box 1
Rapidan, Virginia 22733

First Edition Published in 1946 by Allen Walker
Revised in 1953 by Southern Publishing Association
Published 1985 by Amazing Facts Incorporated
Edited by Dennis Crews
Published 2001 by Hartland Publications with added appendix
Edited by Charles Tompkins

Printed in U.S.A.

ISBN 0-923309-69-1

The Law
and
The Sabbath

Chapter

Foreword to the 1985 Edition

Forty years have not dimmed my meories of the man who became the role model for my own evangelistic ministry. For one thing my mother-in-law would not let me forget Allen Walker. She spoke often of that bold, self-educated, southern evangelist who had introduced her to Christ and His message in a tent revival soon after she was married.

Later as an aspiring young evangelist in Florida, I heard other ministers speak almost reverently about the spiritual exploits of Allen Walker. His fantastic knowledge of the Scriptures, a fearless nature, and unassailable logic made him almost a legend through the southland where he conducted protracted evangelistic "efforts."

By my second public crusade in 1950 he was retired, yet he still had a daily radio program operating in Dothan, Alabama, just a few miles from Tallahassee, Florida where I was pastoring. I made it a point to visit with him at every possible opportunity, plying him with questions about soul-winning. He welcomed my visits and patiently endured my enthusiastic interrogations.

I listened spellbound to his accounts of old-fashioned platform "debates" with combative ministers who soufht to neutralize his evangelistic influence. In the days when such public exchanges were considered a normal part of "fighting the good fight," he quietly and kindly, with text after text, silenced every opponent to his powerful preaching of the Sabbath.

A strange bond of affection grew between us—the seasoned veteran and the greenhorn youth. For two years I had the privilege of sitting at the feet of that great and humble man. When LuAnn and I responded to a mission call to India in 1952, we felt quite sure that our friend would not survive the five-year term of our separation. The sad news came to us in faraway Bangalore that Allen Walker had died in the harness of his beloved evangelism.

During those early 1950s in Tallahassee, every one of my young friends in the ministry had a well-worn copy of Walker's paperbound book, *The Law and the Sabbath*. It was his own fascinating recital of dialogues with preachers of many persuasions who had challenged his teaching on the subject of Sabbathkeeping. I still have that beat-up unabridged version from which I memorized literally scores of texts and their exegeses.

When the paperback was finally recognized for its true value, the Southern Publishing Association printed a revised clothbound edition which became almost like a second Bible to hundreds of young evangelists and pastors.

For over twenty years this treasured volume has been out of print. Those who were fortunate enough to own one have preserved it with loving care. When I first learned that it was not going to be reprinted, I bought every copy available in the bookstores—seventeen in all, if I remember correctly. During the intervening years I have shared those wonderful books with young preachers whom I have helped to train for the ministry.

Today the arguments against the truth which constrained my friend Allen Wlker to write his masterpiece are being leveled once more against the law of God. My supply of the books disappeared long ago. There is a desperate need for Sabbathkeeping Christians to learn how to defend their faith and practice against those who would annihilate or neutralize the great moral law of God's Ten Commandments. For this reason Amazing Facts is delighted to present this newly-revised, long-awaited book by a stalwart defender of the faith. May it bring the same blessing to every reader as it has brought to me during the thirty-eight years of my ministry.

Joe Crews
Director, Amazing Facts
July, 1985

CHAPTER 1

Why We Cannot Be Justified by Works

PERHAPS no charge is brought against Sabbathkeepers more frequently than that they teach salvation by the works of the law. They are called legalists and are accused by some of ignoring the great gospel truth of salvation by grace through faith. Others persistently say that they mix law and grace and depend on a little bit of each to earn their way into the kingdom of heaven. Actually, nothing could be further from the truth.

I once invited a Moody Bible Institute preacher to attend church with me one Sabbath morning to hear a sermon on righteousness and justification by faith. He accepted the invitation, and as he sat and listened, he acted as though he could scarcely believe his ears. For years he had been teaching orally and in his tracts and pamphlets that Sabbathkeepers depend on "works of the law" to merit favor with God in order to be saved. The sermon was so different from what he had been teaching that at the close of the service he expressed amazement at hearing such a beautiful and balanced presentation of the gospel. This revealed exactly what I had expected: he had been misinformed. And the same thing is true of the great majority of those who oppose and speak against Sabbathkeeping Christians.

In Job 25:4 the question is asked: "How then can man be justified with God?" So much is involved in the right answer that everyone should be interested in the biblical teaching concerning it. Are there any provisions for justification except through Christ and the blood atonement? Paul says, "Therefore being justified by faith, we have peace with God through our Lord Jesus Christ." Romans 5:1.

Has there ever been any other way of being justified before God? Were men before the cross justified "by the works of the law" and since the cross "by grace"? Are such divisions scriptural? If men in Old Testament times were saved by works, why did God after the cross change His plan and put men under a plan of salvation "by grace"? Can a single scripture be cited to prove that any man between Adam and John the Baptist was "saved" by his own works of righteousness? Will those who so persistently claim that in those days it was "the dispensation of salvation by works" point out the verse which says that any man then or since was saved by "works of the law"?

There are some other questions to be considered: After a man stands before God "justified by faith," what will be the attitude of his heart and mind toward the Ten Commandments? Will he boast that since he is "justified by faith," and not "by the works of the law," this gives him license to steal, lie, violate the Sabbath, murder, and break the other commandments? If a man cannot be justified "by the works of the law," is there some good reason why this is impossible? These are some of the questions that will be examined in the light of the Scriptures. May the Lord give the reader an honest heart and a love for the truth as he continues to read this book.

"How then can man be justified with God?" What does the word "justified" mean? As used by Paul, "justification" means just the opposite of "condemnation." Romans 5:1 reads, "Therefore being justified by faith, we have peace with God through our Lord Jesus Christ." Since that is the case, Romans 8:1 is also true: "There is therefore now no condemnation to them which are in Christ Jesus." The unjustified man stands before God under condemnation. The justified man stands before God free from condemnation. Through Adam "judgment came upon all men to condemnation"; and through Christ "the free gift came upon all men unto justification." Romans 5:18. These statements taken together show that "justification" is the opposite of "condemnation."

The unjustified man is "under the law," that is, under its condemnation. He is "guilty before God." Romans 3:19 proves that this is true: "Now we know that what things soever the law saith, it saith to them who are under the law: that every mouth may be stopped, and all the world may become guilty before God." This text makes it plain that "under the law" means "under the condemnation of the law because of transgression," and this makes all unjustified persons guilty before God. The question now is, "How are such to become right in the sight of God?" As long as man stands guilty before God, he is still under condemnation and is lost in God's sight.

It is impossible to comprehend the doctrine of justification by faith without understanding the doctrine of sin. This is so, for it is because of sin that man stands guilty before God and in need of justification. If sin had never come into the world, all would stand justified before God and free from condemnation.

The Truth About Sin

What is sin? Nothing could be defined more understandably. Here are a few texts: "Whosoever committeth sin transgresseth also the law: for sin is the transgression of the law." 1 John 3:4. "For by the law is the knowledge of sin." Romans 3:20. "I had not known sin, but by the law. For I had not known lust, except the law had said, Thou shalt not covet." Romans 7:7. "For where no law is, there is no transgression." Romans 4:15. "But sin is not imputed when there is no law." Romans 5:13. "The strength of sin is the law." 1 Corinthians 15:56.

One of the plainest doctrines of the New Testament is that "sin is the transgression of the law" of the Ten Commandments. It was the law which said, "Thou shalt not covet," that revealed to Paul exactly what sin is (Romans 7:7).

Since all have sinned (Romans 3:23), since the wages of sin is death (Romans 6:23), and since death passed upon all men (Romans 5:12), it is clear that the whole human race is condemned by the law. Man stands guilty before God, and in need of justification. God's act of justification releases man from this guilt and condemnation. He stands before God and the law accounted as innocent, even as was Adam before he sinned, and as Christ when He challenged His enemies, "Which of you convinceth me of sin?" But it will be seen that in providing for this degree of justification, through what Christ has done for the sinner, God does not do away with the violated law. He will not cancel the law to accommodate the transgressor; but through the sufferings of Christ in man's behalf He instead cancels the death sentence under which the violated law holds the sinner.

If a man is condemned by the civil law for stealing, the law is not abolished by the state so that there will be nothing to testify to his guilt. If the law were abolished, it would grant license to him and all other thieves. The same thing is true concerning the Ten Commandments, for "sin is not imputed when there is no law." Romans 5:13. It is plain, therefore, that any doctrine of justification which would abolish the law that brought the transgressor under its condemnation is not the doctrine of justification; for Paul inquires, "Do we then make void the law through faith?" His answer is, "God forbid: yea, we establish the law." Romans 3:31.

The doctrine of justification by faith must uphold the just claim of the law against the transgressor and at the same time take care of his penalty. Simply to do away with the violated law would be saying that it was an unjust law in the first place and never should have been brought into existence. It would be saying that the man was just and the law which condemned him was unjust. But God is the author of the Ten Commandments, and He cannot be charged with the folly of putting into operation a law that was so unjust that it would be wrong to hold the transgressor guilty for violating it. Erring man may make the mistake of doing such a thing, but not the God of heaven. The Holy Spirit says that God's law, which man has violated, is "holy, and just, and good" (Romans 7:12).

Works Cannot Save

The fact that man cannot be justified "by the works of the law" is easily seen from a study of the following verses:

"Therefore by the deeds of the law there shall no flesh be justified in his sight. . . . Therefore we conclude that a man is justified by faith without the deeds of the law." Romans 3:20,28. "Knowing that a man is not justified by the works of the law, but by the faith of Jesus Christ, even we have believed in Jesus Christ, that we might be justified by the faith of Christ, and not by the works of the law: for by the works of the law shall no flesh be justified. . . . I do not frustrate the grace of God: for if righteousness come by the law, then Christ is dead in vain." Galatians 2:16,21.

Let's take a brief look at just what the violation of the law has gotten man into, and why that law cannot get him out of his predicament. Romans 3:23 states that "all have sinned." What is sin? "Sin is the transgression of the law." 1 John 3:4. What is the penalty for transgression? "The wages of sin is death." Romans 6:23. Since "all have sinned," how many are under the death sentence? "So death passed upon all men, for that all have sinned." Romans 5:12.

Think about it this way: if any man would undertake to justify himself, he must first acknowledge that he has sinned and is under the sentence of death. Next he must die to pay the just penalty of the law. Having paid his own penalty by his death, he must next raise himself from the dead. Having done that, he can stand before the law as an uncondemned man, justified by the works which he has done for himself.

If man could pay his own penalty by dying and raising himself, and then live a sinless life under the same conditions Jesus experienced, he could then stand before the law without being condemned, and God would even owe him a debt of eternal life. But since everyone understands the utter impossibility of this, what folly it would be for any Christian to believe and teach righteousness by works!

When a man is put into a state prison for one year to pay the penalty for the violation of some state law, he remains under the law—that is, under its judicial condemnation—until the penalty is paid. When the last day of his sentence has expired, he walks away and is no longer under the law, that is, under the condemnation of the law, because his works have paid the stated penalty. Then, through his own works, he stands justified in the presence of the law. This could be called justification by works. If the penalty had been death, however, no amount of works would have paid the penalty—only death itself would suffice.

This illustration explains why none who have violated the divine law can be justified by works. The penalty is death, not works. Every Christian should understand that man cannot be justified by works, and should also understand why he cannot. Man cannot work off a death penalty and restore himself to life again.

The New Testament declares that "by the deeds of the law there shall no flesh be justified in his sight" (Romans 3:20). This is because "all have sinned," and "sin is the transgression of the law." This brings every transgressor "under the law"—under its judicial condemnation. In view of this, how can a violated law witness to the innocence of a transgressor? It cannot, of course. It would be witnessing to a lie. Heaven's charge is that all have sinned. A perfect mirror cannot witness that a mechanic's face, smeared with grease and dirt, is clean. It is just as impossible for a violated law to testify that its transgressor is guiltless. To smash the mirror would not clean the mechanic's face; neither can man's attempt to do away with the law cleanse him from the defilement of sin or pay the penalty for his transgression, both of which are necessarily involved in bringing about his justification. The angels of heaven could stand beside the law, and it would have to witness to their innocence because they have not transgressed it. It would have to testify to their purity. The same can be said of Jesus. His challenge was, "Which of you convinceth me of sin?" But since all other men have transgressed the law, it condemns all—and justifies none.

Since man's violation of the Decalogue makes it impossible for the law to witness to his justification, one can easily understand the meaning of the following scriptures:

"Therefore by the deeds of the law there shall no flesh be justified in his sight: for by the law is the knowledge of sin." Romans 3:20.

"Therefore we conclude that a man is justified by faith without the deeds of the law." Romans 3:28.

"Knowing that a man is not justified by the works of the law, but by the faith of Jesus Christ, even we have believed in Jesus Christ, that we might be justified by the faith of Christ, and not by the works of the law: for by the works of the law shall no flesh be justified." Galatians 2:16.

"For as many as are of the works of the law are under the curse. . . . No man is justified by the law in the sight of God, it is evident: for, The just shall live by faith." Galatians 3:10,11.

"Christ is become of no effect unto you, whosoever of you are justified by the law; ye are fallen from grace." Galatians 5:4.

Christians who understand the Word of God strongly hold the truths of these inspired texts. But at the same time they avoid the dangerous conclusion that these texts abolish the law of God and therefore they can steal, murder, desecrate the Sabbath day, and practice with impunity the other sins condemned by it.

Justification No License for Sin

Although the Apostle Paul was firm in his insistence that no man who has violated the Ten Commandments can ever hope to be justified by them, at the same time he carefully guarded against adopting one idea some have gathered by a misunderstanding of his words. Some people feel that justification by faith issues a permit to practice the sins which the law condemns. In Galatians 2:16, where he declares that a man is not justified by the works of the law, the Holy Spirit guided him to clarify the point in the very next verse: "But if, while we seek to be justified by Christ, we ourselves also are found sinners, is therefore Christ the minister of sin? God forbid." Galatians 2:17.

These two verses can be summed up as follows:

Although we cannot be justified by the law, we should never conclude that faith in Jesus Christ gives us license to violate it willfully.

In fact, Paul goes on to say that if he did willfully violate it, he would make himself a transgressor. He then states, "For I through the law am dead to the law, that I might live unto God." Galatians 2:19.

Because the law condemned him when he saw its spiritual significance, Paul was led to Christ for justification; thus beginning with the law, he had at last become dead to the law—that is, judicially dead—and to its penalty of death. Jesus' death had satisfied the claims of the violated law in his behalf. This favor had come to him through faith. Paul enlarges upon this thought in Galatians 3:22,23: "But the scripture hath concluded all under sin, that the promise by faith of Jesus Christ might be given to them that believe. But before faith came, we were kept under the law, shut up unto the faith which should afterwards be revealed."

In these verses the expression "under sin" means being under the condemnation of sin. "Under the law" means being under the condemnation of the law. As soon as Paul received Christ by faith, there came a release from this condition. Before this personal exercise of faith he was shut up in prison, held there because of the violation of the law. So Paul was not talking dispensationally, but experimentally. He was not speaking of conditions which existed after Calvary in contrast with those conditions which existed before the cross. He was speaking of his standing as an individual after exercising the "faith of Jesus Christ" as contrasted with his personal "shut-up" condition before the exercise of this releasing faith in Jesus Christ.

Paul points out the fact that the justified man will "live unto God," not through his own efforts, but because Christ lives in him (Galatians 2:19,20). Christ through the Holy Spirit lives in the justified person, "that the righteousness of the law might be fulfilled" in him (Romans 8:4).

It is a sad mistake to teach that the doctrine of justification does away with the law and gives the one justified license to violate it. This has been taught so widely and aggressively that it has bred contempt for God's holy law. Countless thousands of sincere Christians have been left with the impression that it is possible to be rewarded with justification by despising the law and everything for which it stands. Paul was uncompromising in his insistence that the doctrine of justification, in its true setting and application, made no provision for holding the Ten Commandments in contempt, or for thinking that one could merit favor with God by a life of disobedience to them.

Thus far this study into the proposition of how a man cannot be justified has led to the conclusion that no man can be justified by works or by the law. Since it has also been found that the New Testament doctrine of justification has made no provision for the abolition of the law or for *willful* transgression thereof, the next logical question is this: What is the law for? And what is the relationship of a fully justified person to its demands?

The Purpose of the Law

Paul tells us plainly that "by the law is the knowledge of sin." Romans 3:20. In another place he spoke of a law which says, "Thou shalt not covet," and of course this law is the Decalogue. He said, "I had not known sin, but by the law." Romans 7:7. This repeats what he said before: "By the law is the knowledge of sin." If it is true that "by the law is the knowledge of sin," then it is also true that "sin is the transgression of the law." 1 John 3:4. Law is so related to transgression that "where no law is, there is no transgression." Romans 4:15.

If we do away with the law, we destroy the possibility of transgression, and at the same time remove the possibility of condemnation. When we do away with the possibility of condemnation, we annul both the necessity of the atonement and the need of justification. So "the law entered [in written form], that the offence might abound" (Romans 5:20), which is the same as saying that "by the law is the knowledge of sin."

The law is the great sin detector, and when men find themselves confronted by the certain penalty for its violation, the unfathomable love of God directs their attention to the Sufferer of Calvary, of whom it is said, "He shall save his people from their sins." Matthew 1:21. On the other hand, if it can be shown that the law is null and void, then there is no such thing as sin and, consequently, no need of a Saviour.

It is the purpose of the law to reveal what sin is. This explains, perhaps more than any other reason, why Sabbathkeeping Christians observe the seventh day. It has already been pointed out that Paul said that sin was the transgression of the law which reads, "Thou shalt not covet." It is scripturally certain that this same law also states, "Remember the sabbath day, to keep it holy," and adds, "The seventh day is the sabbath of the Lord thy God." How can it be contended that it is sinful to break the tenth commandment (regarding covetousness) but not sinful to violate the fourth commandment of the same law respecting the observance of the Lord's holy Sabbath day?

In Ephesians 6:2,3 Paul said, "Honour thy father and mother; which is the first commandment with promise; that it may be well with thee, and thou mayest live long on the earth." Here Paul quotes the fifth commandment of the Decalogue. Was Paul teaching legalism—salvation by works of the law? Or was he teaching that Christian children, as well as adult Christians, should respect and obey the commandments?

When Sabbathkeeping Christians encourage people to respect the seventh day, it is charged that they are teaching legalism and salvation by works. In reply to this charge it may be asked, Was Paul teaching the same thing when he said that children should respect their parents, and when he quoted one of the Ten Commandments as a reason why they should do this? The same arguments that would condemn Sabbathkeepers with reference to the fourth commandment would condemn Paul with reference to the fifth.

How Can Man Be Justified?

Certainly with a violated law condemning him, and a sentence of death resting upon him, man is entangled in such a helpless state that it's easy to see the force of the question: "How then can man be justified with God?" And yet justification is possible, irrespective of the past, as we will soon see.

When Paul went to Corinth to proclaim the glad tidings of God's redeeming grace, his audience contained adulterers, thieves, drunkards, idolaters, and those who were guilty of sins too revolting to mention (1 Corinthians 6:9,10). Then speaking of the change which had come into their lives, he said: "But ye are washed, but ye are sanctified, but ye are justified in the name of the Lord Jesus, and by the Spirit of our God."

Here is the joyful news that justification is a possibility! No one needs to be in despair and say, "I have been so ruined by sin that there is no hope for me." But the question, "How?" is still unanswered. The only way out is for someone to come to the rescue. This person must take the penalty for sin. Is there one who will do this for the condemned man? If so, who is he? Man cannot die for man because every man is already under his own death sentence. "Death passed upon all men, for that all have sinned." Romans 5:12. The substitute must be one whose life is equal in value to all lives forfeited.

This One is the blessed Jesus! Since it is through Him that "we live, and move, and have our being," He is thus the source of all life; His life is more than equal in value to every life forfeited, for all are dependent upon Him for their existence.

It can now be seen that justification depends upon what God does for man instead of what man can do for himself through his own works. Isaiah 53:11 reads, "By his knowledge shall my righteous servant [Christ] justify many; for he shall bear their iniquities."

"How then can man be justified with God?" The answer is: His beloved Son takes man's place, suffering in his stead. Paul says, "Christ died for our sins." 1 Corinthians 15:3. By dying Christ paid the penalty which the broken law imposed, and thus released the sinner from that penalty. When a sinful man by faith accepts what Christ has done for him, he is no longer under judicial condemnation of the law. The penalty for past transgression no longer hangs over his head. It has been paid by another. This is what Paul means when he says: "For I . . . am dead to the law, that I might live unto God." Galatians 2:19. And, "Christ hath redeemed us from the curse of the law, being made a curse for us: for it is written, Cursed is every one that hangeth on a tree." Galatians 3:13.

The curse of the law is the penalty of death, which "passed upon all men" (Romans 5:12). If man were left to pay this penalty, he would perish in the second death; but "God so loved the world, that he gave his only begotten Son, that whosoever believeth in him should not perish, but have everlasting life." John 3:16.

The expression "hangeth upon a tree" has reference to Jesus' death on the cross. The word "redeemed" has reference to something which had been previously mortgaged. Through transgression man mortgaged his life beyond the limit of his power to redeem. Only death could cancel the mortgage, for "the wages of sin is death." Romans 6:23. Man could not redeem his mortgaged life by works; the price was death. This curse of the law rested upon him, and the only hope was for another to redeem him from the curse of this death penalty by paying the redemptive price for him, which Christ did when He died on Calvary.

The provision for man's justification was made through Christ's dying in his stead, thus sanctioning the justice of the penalty which the broken law imposed, and at the same time redeeming man from the penalty which he had brought upon himself through transgression. What part does man have in obtaining justification? All that is required of man is brought out in Romans 5:1: "Therefore being justified by faith, we have peace with God through our Lord Jesus Christ."

By faith man, in accepting Christ, appropriates the provisions and the benefits of the Lord's death; and in so doing he passes from a state of condemnation to a state of justification. It is all of faith and none of works. It has always been difficult for the gospel teacher to bring people to see and accept this great truth. Men feel that they must have some part in working out their justification, that their own good works must be thrown in with what Christ has done, and that these works must count for something. The lesson must be learned that it is by faith, and by faith alone, that justification comes. This is what the Scriptures teach, and it is the only hope for man's salvation.

Chapter 2

Righteousness By Faith

So far we have not gone into the meaning of righteousness by faith, but have only given evidence that Sabbathkeepers understand that righteousness is of faith, and not of works. We shall now consider the great and precious truth, which Paul speaks of as "the righteousness of the law . . . fulfilled in us." Romans 8:4.

Christ's Righteousness

Christ is the only sinless one who ever lived upon this earth. His righteousness was without a flaw; there was nothing in His life which the Ten Commandments could condemn. He alone could say, "Which of you convinceth me of sin?" John 8:46. Paul tells us that Christ was "without sin" (Hebrews 4:15). Peter declares that Christ "did no sin" (1 Peter 2:22). God's gracious arrangement for man is that the perfect righteousness of Christ is imputed to him who believes. This righteousness is credited to the believer just as though he had lived that life. This righteousness is offered freely, and, when accepted, it becomes righteousness by faith. That is what Paul means when he says, "We shall be saved by his life." Romans 5:10. There is nothing in *that* life that can be condemned. If we are credited with it, we cannot be condemned in the judgment, and we shall pass into the kingdom of God, saved by Christ's life.

There are several scriptures to prove this point. Here is one: "They which receive . . . the gift of righteousness shall reign in life by one, Jesus Christ." Romans 5:17. Righteousness is something we receive as a gift, not something that we work out for ourselves. On this point Paul says: "Now to him that worketh is the reward not reckoned of grace, but of debt. But to him that worketh not, but believeth on him that justifieth the ungodly, his faith is counted for righteousness." Romans 4:4,5.

We read in Romans 5:18: "Therefore as by the offence of one [Adam] judgment came upon all men to condemnation; even so by the righteousness of one [Christ] the free gift [of righteousness] came upon all men unto justification of life.

This text makes it plain that the righteousness by which we are saved is the righteousness of Christ, a free gift received by faith. This is righteousness by faith. The next verse says, "For as by one man's disobedience many were made sinners, so by the obedience of one shall many be made [accounted] righteous."

We are accounted righteous by receiving by faith the obedience of Christ. The Scriptures teach that Christ exchanged with us. He took the blame for our life of sin and disobedience, in which He experimentally had no part, and paid the penalty in our stead. In exchange we get credit for His life of obedience and sinlessness, in which we experimentally had no part, and we receive the reward of eternal life. This is one of the most blessed truths that God has revealed to man.

Always Righteousness by Faith

This phase of the subject has been presented quite fully in order to guard against the deceptive teaching that before the cross it was all law and no grace, and since the cross it has been all grace and no law. Man has always been prone to go to extremes in dealing with fundamental truths. In the days of Jesus the slogan of popular religion was "Up with the law and down with grace"; today it is "Up with grace and down with the law." The fact is that both law and grace have always played specific roles in the plan of redemption—the *law* to point out what sin is, and *grace* to save from sin. Preaching the truth does away with neither; it merely places each in its divinely appointed setting and does not emphasize one to the destruction of the other.

Since "God is no respecter of persons" (Acts 10:34), and since His plan of salvation for man has always been the same, righteousness by faith prevailed in the Old Testament times. Speaking of Abraham, Paul says, "Abraham believed God, and it [this faith] was counted unto him for righteousness. . . . Faith was reckoned to Abraham for righteousness." Romans 4:3,9. This is righteousness by faith. Further in the chapter we read: "He staggered not at the promise of God through unbelief; but was strong in faith, giving glory to God; and being fully persuaded that, what he had promised, he was able also to perform. And therefore it [this faith] was imputed to him for righteousness." Romans 4:20–22.

God did not, in the days of Abraham, place men on a regime of working out their own righteousness, for that would have been just as impossible for them as for us. God's provision has always been righteousness by faith. The next verses jump from Abraham's day to Paul's and to ours, and say: "Now it was not written for his sake alone, that it was imputed to him; but for us also. . . . if we believe on him that raised up Jesus our Lord from the dead." Romans 4:23,24.

The Penalty of Sin

Before a person is convicted of sin by the Holy Spirit, before he has found pardon and justification in Christ, he faces the penalty for sin. But in accepting Christ, he is released and made free from that penalty because Christ paid it for him.

Let us next consider the first seven verses of Romans 7. They have to do with being "delivered" from the penalty of the law through the atonement provided by the death of Jesus on the cross. The first verse reads: "Know ye not, brethren, (for I speak to them that know the law,) how that the law hath dominion over a man as long as he liveth?"

This demonstrates that Paul was not going to teach that this law had become "dead" and was no longer operative against the transgressor. For how could a "dead" law have "dominion" over a man? When a man claims that because he has become "justified by faith" he is "above law" and can steal, lie, commit adultery, or live in violation of any of the other commandments without forfeiting his justification and returning to a state of condemnation, he is only deceiving himself. Of this Paul says, "Be not deceived; neither fornicators, nor idolaters, nor adulterers, . . . nor thieves, nor covetous, . . . shall inherit the kingdom of God." 1 Corinthians 6:9,10. We may be sure there is nothing in the seventh chapter of Romans or any other part of the Bible contrary to this.

The second verse continues this thought: "For the woman which hath an husband is bound by the law [of faithfulness and fidelity] to her husband so long as he liveth." As long as this husband lives, she is to keep herself "only to him" as she promised in the marriage vow; but if he dies, she does no wrong in marrying another man. In this analogy it was the "husband" and not the "law" that died. "But if the husband be dead, she is loosed from the law [of fidelity] of her husband." It is the husband that dies. "So then if, while her husband liveth, she be married to another man, she shall be called an adulteress" (verse three); for in so doing, she violates two laws: (1) that of fidelity, which she owed to her husband, and (2) the seventh commandment, which forbids adultery. "But if her husband be dead [not either of these laws], she is free from that law [of fidelity]; so that she is no adulteress, though she be married to another man."

Here are three things: (1) the woman, (2) the law, and (3) the husband. Which of these three died?

1. "If the woman be dead"—that is not what it says.
2. "If the law be dead"—that is not what it says.
3. "If the husband be dead"—that is what it says.

How pleasing it would be to the no-law teachers if it read, "But if the law be dead." That is what they are trying to prove, but it does not read that way.

"Wherefore, my brethren, ye also are become dead to the law." Romans 7:4. It does not say, "The law has become dead," but, "Ye . . . are become dead." "Ye also are become dead to the law"—to the judicial penalty of the law to which they were bound as the woman to the husband. "Ye also are become dead to the law by the body of Christ." Notice the words "by the body of Christ." This expression means "by the death of Christ on the cross." Peter says, "Who his own self bare our sins in his own body on the tree." 1 Peter 2:24. Now let us ask ourselves, Did Jesus' death on the cross cancel the law, or the death penalty—which? Paul says that Christ "by the grace of God should taste death for every man." Hebrews 2:9. Why did He taste death for every man? Because "death passed upon all men." Romans 5:12. So Christ's death was to cancel the penalty—not the law itself.

In Paul's analogy, when the woman who has been "married" to this sentence of "death" (which is true of all of us) receives Christ, she is then and there "loosed" from that sentence (husband) and married to another, even Christ. If we continue in our transgression, if we willfully violate the Sabbath commandment every week, or any other commandment, we are still "bound" to that husband of "death." So if while we are living in this transgression, we claim we are married to Christ, such a life is one of spiritual adultery.

Having been liberated from the "death which passed upon all men," we are, at the same time, "discharged from the law." Romans 7:6, A.S.V. This text does not imply that we are free to steal, lie, commit adultery, murder, etc., but that we are discharged from the death sentence "by the body of Christ." As Paul goes on to explain, "That being dead wherein we were held." The American Standard Version reads, "Having died to that wherein we were held." The fact that this release was accomplished by the body of Christ proves it was the death that passed upon all men which becomes judicially dead when a person accepts the gospel. He becomes "discharged from the law."

"Discharged From the Law"

These words, "discharged from the law," are legal terms. A man pays another man's penalty, and the judge says to the prisoner, "You are discharged, sir." He does not mean discharged to go out and violate the law again, but discharged from the penalty. So on the cross Christ paid our penalty and thus made it possible for us to be discharged from the law as far as its death penalty was concerned. Then we become dead "to that wherein we were held," namely, the death penalty. Our allegiance to that "husband" has terminated because he became dead "by the body of Christ." Then we become "married to another, even to him who is raised from the dead, that we should bring forth fruit unto God."

In order to make it plain that he was not arguing that the law is "dead," and no longer operative against the transgressor, Paul goes on to say, "What shall we say then? Is the law sin? God forbid. Nay, I had not known sin, but by the law: for I had not known lust, except the law had said, Thou shalt not covet." Romans 7:7. How could any commandment of a dead law condemn a living man for violating it? Such a thing would be impossible. But the very fact that Paul quotes the tenth commandment of the Sinai law and goes on to say that it is this law that reveals a knowledge of sin—this positively proves it would be equally true of the fourth or any other commandment of the Decalogue. Stephen, preaching this side of the cross, said: "This is he [Moses] that was in the church in the wilderness with the angel which spake to him in the mount Sina, and with our fathers: who received the lively [living, A.S.V.] oracles to give unto us." Acts 7:38. So these Ten Commandments given on Mount Sinai were "living" and not "dead." All who are willfully violating them, while at the same time claiming they are married to Christ, are living in spiritual adultery.

The theory that justification by faith, as taught in the New Testament, makes void the law and gives license to disobey the commandments of

God has back of it one single aim: to evade the observance of the Lord's holy Sabbath day. But since this faith by which the sinner is justified does not make void the law, but establishes it, the Sabbath is also established, since it is part of the law.

Right and Wrong Ways

We now come to the bible truth about righteousness by faith. Justification has to do with man's deliverance from the penalty of the law, which is death. Righteousness has to do with man's being reckoned in harmony with "the righteousness of the law" so that he stands "accepted in the beloved." (Romans 8:4; Ephesians 1:6). Man is just as powerless to *work out* the righteousness demanded by the law as he was to *work off* its penalty.

Since God's plan for justifying the sinner does not make void the law or grant license to disobey God's commandments; since even a justified man cannot, of himself, attain to "the righteousness of the law"; and since "the unrighteous shall not inherit the kingdom of God" (1 Corinthians 6:9), the way of attaining to a standard of righteousness that the law cannot condemn becomes a vital question. In fact our entering into the kingdom of God depends upon the proper answer.

There is a right and a wrong way of going about it. The wrong way is thus described: "But Israel, which followed after the law of righteousness, hath not attained to the law of righteousness. Wherefore? Because they sought it not by faith, but as it were by the works of the law." Romans 9:31,32.

The right way to attain to the righteousness demanded by the law is found in Romans 9:30: "The Gentiles, which followed not after righteousness, have attained to righteousness, even the righteousness which is of faith."

The wrong way is righteousness by human attempt. The right way is righteousness which is of faith. Israel's wrong way was "going about to establish their own righteousness." Romans 10:3. The right way is to let Christ, through the Holy Spirit, dwell in us, "that the righteousness of the law might be fulfilled in us." Romans 8:4. The wrong way is *by* us, the right way is *in* us. This necessary righteousness is "not of works, lest any man should boast" (Ephesians 2:9), but just the opposite, for "God imputeth righteousness without works" (Romans 4:6). The righteousness which God accepts is not self-manufactured, but divinely imputed. It is not accomplished "by works of righteousness which we have done" (Titus 3:5), but by "the righteousness of God which is by faith of Jesus Christ unto all and upon all them that believe" (Romans 3:22). One is not saved by keeping the law, but he obeys because he is saved.

A book on the life of Christ written by a well-known Sabbathkeeping author states this truth beautifully:

"The fountain of the heart must be purified before the streams can become pure. He who is trying to reach heaven by his own works in keeping the law is attempting an impossibility. . . . The Christian's life is not a modification or improvement of the old, but a transformation of nature. There is a death to self and sin, and a new life altogether. This change can be brought about only by the effectual working of the Holy Spirit." *The Desire of Ages*, p. 172.

In another book by the same author we read:

"The thought that the righteousness of Christ is imputed to us, not because of any merit on our part, but as a free gift from God, is a precious thought. The enemy of God and man is not willing that this truth should be clearly presented; for he knows that if the people receive it fully, his power will be broken." *Gospel Workers*, p. 161.

We could offer many more quotations, but what has been said should be sufficient to convince any honest heart that Sabbathkeeping Christians do not believe in righteousness by works. They firmly believe that salvation is by faith alone; that justification is by faith alone; that righteousness is by faith alone; and this is their true position before the people of every nation, tongue, and kindred in the world.

A noted evangelist was making it a special point to charge that people who observe the Sabbath teach righteousness by works. Finally one day he became acquainted with the actual beliefs held by the people against whom he was preaching. Very much surprised, he asked: "What do you do with the law, then?" It seemed to him that the doctrine of righteousness by faith implies that the Ten Commandments were made void. This seems to be the idea of all who teach that the seventh day should not now be observed. The no-law theory is the very thing Paul anticipated, and he made haste to correct it. After having said in Romans 3:23 that all had violated the law, and that "by the deeds of the law there shall no flesh be justified in his sight" (verse 20), and that both justification and righteousness are of faith, he adds, "Do we then make void the law through faith?

God forbid: yea, we establish the law." Romans 3:31.

The answer to the question, "If we obtain righteousness by faith, what do we do with the law?" is this: According to Romans 8:3,4, "the righteousness of the law" is "fulfilled in us" through Christ. Paul said in Galatians 2:20, "Christ liveth in me." If Christ, through the Holy Spirit, lives in us, we will certainly not live lives of immorality and lawlessness; for Christ dwells in the heart so that "the righteousness of the law might be fulfilled in us, who walk not after the flesh, but after the Spirit." Thus Christ is everything. He becomes our justification, our righteousness, and our obedience. Any theory of righteousness by faith which teaches that we make void the law through faith, and that Christ is the minister of disobedience, is certainly not the New Testament doctrine of righteousness by faith.

It is not enough to understand intellectually this gracious arrangement for our justification and salvation. We must by prayer enter into a definite faith transaction with God and appropriate pardon, justification, and righteousness. We may have a knowledge that food will keep us from starvation; but unless we receive this food, it will not save us from death. Just so, we may know that Jesus has died for our offenses and was raised for our justification; we may be able to understand and explain all the principles of the Bible concerning justification and righteousness by faith, but unless we, by prayer and faith, appropriate what Christ has done for us, and then trust Him daily to the end, it will not benefit us.

Look upon Jesus, sinless is He;
Father, impute His life unto me.
My life of scarlet, my sin and woe,
Cover with His life, whiter than snow.

Deep are the wounds transgression has made;
Red are the stains; my soul is afraid.
O to be covered, Jesus, with Thee,
Safe from the law that now judgeth me!

Longing the joy of pardon to know,
Jesus hold out a robe white as snow;

"Lord, I accept it! leaving my own,
Gladly I wear Thy pure life alone."

Reconciled by His death for my sin,
Justified by His life pure and clean,
Sanctified by obeying His word,
Glorified when returneth my Lord.

——F. E. Belden

Chapter 3

Is Obedience Legalism?

One thing is very noticeable about those who write and preach against the seventh-day Sabbath. It is this: When most evangelical ministers or commentators say anything about the enduring nature of the Ten Commandments and the importance of obedience to them, it is considered "sound doctrine." But let a Sabbathkeeping minister make the same statements, and he is immediately accused of teaching legalism and salvation by the works of the law. Such an attitude reveals only how quickly some people succumb to prejudice. Let us turn to what ministers of other denominations have said about the eternity of the commandments and the importance of obedience to them.

Teachings of Other Churches

Dwight L. Moody wrote a book on the Ten Commandments entitled *Weighed and Wanting.* This is what he said about the law: "The commandments of God given to Moses in the mount at Horeb are as binding today as ever they have been since the time when they were proclaimed in the hearing of the people." —p. 15. Many have been the times when a Sabbathkeeping minister made a similar statement, and immediately he was branded as a teacher of legalism, Galatianism, and salvation by the works of the law. What is very strange is that when Moody makes the statement, he is regarded as teaching the truth.

On page 16 Moody declares, "The people must be made to understand that the Ten Commandments are still binding, and that there is a penalty attached to their violation."

Here is what Moody says about the Sabbath commandment: "I honestly believe that this commandment is just as binding today as it ever was. I have talked with men who have said it was abrogated, but they have never been able to point to any place in the bible where God repealed it. When Christ was on earth, He did nothing to set it aside." —p. 46.

In *The Sunday School Times* of October 17, 1948, H. A. Ironside said, "The law of Ten Commandments has to do with moral principles, and these are unchanging in any dispensation." That is scriptural, and is precisely what Sabbathkeepers believe. But why is it legalism if they teach it, and "grace" if Ironside teaches it?

In the *Standard Manual of Baptist Churches*, page 66, are these words: "We believe the Scriptures teach that the law of God is the eternal and unchangeable rule of His moral government; that it is holy, just and good. . . . Unfeigned obedience to the holy law is the end [objective] of the gospel." Then on page 61 we read, "We believe that the Scriptures teach that the salvation of sinners is wholly by grace." Now if the Baptists can believe that the Ten Commandment law is eternal and unchangeable and that unfeigned obedience to this law is New Testament doctrine, yet at the same time not do away with the truth that "the salvation of sinners is wholly by grace," why cannot those who love God's holy Sabbath teach and believe the same without being called legalists and false teachers? Are such charges based on Christian honesty and fairness? Are they not purposely calculated to create prejudice?

This unfairness is illustrated in another way. Some ministers do not seem to discover that the Ten Commandments are done away, and that it is legalism to obey them, until they are confronted specifically with the Sabbath issue. As mentioned, when Ironside was commenting on a Sunday school lesson, he said, "The law of Ten Commandments has to do with moral principles, and these are unchanging in any dispensation." (And one of these unchanging commandments declares that "the seventh day is the sabbath of the Lord thy God.") But in another issue of the same paper, and in dealing more directly with the teachings of Sabbathkeepers, Dr. Ironside said, "But the Sabbath of the law was part of that which was done away in Christ at the cross." How could two statements be more contradictory?

In the June, 1946, issue of *Moody Monthly*, page 631, this statement can be found: "The law of God is eternal, never to be abrogated, never set aside. Christ Himself, although we might properly say that He was in reality the Lawgiver and thus had power and authority over the law, indicated His purpose in coming to be that of giving the law its full meaning, and not of destroying it. One could wish that those who profess to be His servants might have the same measure of regard for God's law. If they did, they obviously would not be so ready to ignore it, so quick to change it, or explain it away, and far more ready to accept with their Master every 'jot' and 'tittle.' "

No Sabbathkeeping Christian ever put it more strongly than this. Then why should they be branded legalists, and the writer in *Moody Monthly* be accepted as a teacher of truth since they agree on this point?

Here is an interesting footnote: About the time the quotation just cited came out, the same magazine ran an advertisement of a pamphlet by a Baptist minister against the Sabbath doctrine in which he made bold to say that "Christ on the cross Himself . . . annulled in its entirety, the law of Sinai, the fourth, or Sabbath commandment included." It seems that this writer was very quick to "explain it [the law] away," "change it," and completely "ignore" it. The former writer did not have the seventh-day Sabbath in mind while writing, but the latter did, and there is where the difference always comes in. The persistent question remains: Why should it be called legalism for Sabbathkeepers to teach these things, but grace if others teach them?

The Law Is Spiritual

The Ten Commandments, which Paul speaks of as "the righteousness of the law" to be "fulfilled in us" (Romans 8:4) and not to be willfully violated, are spiritual principles. Paul says, "We know that the law is spiritual." Romans 7:14. Why should one who is spiritual find fault with and oppose that which is spiritual?

The new covenant is this: "I will put my laws into their mid, and write them in their hearts." Hebrews 8:10. That which is spiritual has to do with the heart. If it does not get out of the head into the heart, it is legalism.

Let us remember that it is "the carnal mind" that "is not subject to the law of God." (Romans 8:7). There is no such thing as a carnal mind being in agreement with that which is spiritual. Anyone that rejects the commandments of God and is trying to get them out of the way to justify his transgression of one or all of them is badly infected with carnality, and "to be carnally minded is death" (Romans 8:6).

There are some ministers who insist that when Jesus, in the Sermon on the Mount, spoke of mental "murder" and "adultery," He introduced something new. They go on to say that this could not have been taught in the

Old Testament, that back there people were not actually guilty in the sight of God unless they violated the letter, and that by Jesus' teaching He was setting aside the old commandments for something new. Such teachers are either ignorant themselves or they are trying to deceive in order to justify their opposition to the commandments of God.

By turning to Proverbs 3:1, however, they would find exactly what Jesus taught: "My son, forget not my law; but let thine heart keep my commandments." This text shows that in order to "keep" them in those days the commandments were to be in the heart. David said, "I have inclined mine heart to perform thy statutes." Psalm 119:112. To Samuel it was said, "The Lord looketh on the heart." 1 Samuel 16:7. God has always dealt with man's heart in determining his guilt.

Consequently the Sermon on the Mount was not the introduction of God's dealing with man's heart, but the fulfillment of Isaiah 42:21: "He will magnify the law, and make it honourable." To "magnify" means "to reveal more fully what is already there," and not to add something new. The teachers of Jesus' day had lost sight of the truth stated by Paul that "the law is spiritual." They taught that its legal aspect was at the same time the limit of its spiritual application. When it had been said, "An eye for an eye and a tooth for a tooth," these were purely the civil laws of the nation. They still are in our courts today. The Jewish teachers held that these statutes could be mentally violated without any guilt before God; Jesus, however, taught differently.

Christ magnified the Sabbath commandment along with the others. He said it "was made *for* man" and not *against* him (Mark 2:27). He ignored the petty man-made regulations which had been built up around it, such as the claim that it was wrong to relieve the sick or to feed hungry animals. To Jesus the Sabbath was a sacred institution. Never did He belittle it or say one word against it. All he said about it was in its favor. He did condemn man's ideas of how the Sabbath should be kept, but He never uttered one word which could lead anyone to believe it was a menace to mankind, or that He intended to set it aside. Many orthodox commentators teach the same thing concerning the Sabbath. Too, these truths are taught in the various churches—at least until a sabbatarian evangelist comes into town. It is then that the preachers suddenly discover that the Sabbath was one of the greatest curses ever inflicted upon humanity, that Jesus despised it and did away with it.

True Obedience Motivated by Love

There is nothing that can be termed legalism about the kind of love of which Jesus was speaking when He said: "Thou shalt love the Lord thy God with all thy heart, and with all thy soul, and with all thy mind. This is the first and great commandment. And the second is like unto it, Thou shalt love thy neighbour as thyself. On these two commandments hang all the law and the prophets." Matthew 22:37–40.

Why cannot those who fight God's holy law see that obedience actuated by the warmth of love cannot be legalism? Divine love planted in the heart always manifests itself in obedience. Jesus said, "If ye love me, keep my commandments." John 14:15. And John wrote, "This is the love of God, that we keep his commandments: and his commandments are not grievous." 1 John 5:3. The Goodspeed Translation says, "And his commands are not burdensome." This text shows that if the keeping of God's commandments is burdensome or grievous, our hearts are destitute of the love of God. Why is it that when some hear obedience to the commandments preached, they begin to denounce them, but at the same time glibly talk of "grace, sweet grace" as if the grace of God in the heart meant to despise His commandments?

We wonder whether such a spirit of rebellion against the spiritual law of God is born of the Holy Spirit. We wonder whether that feeling tallies with the statement, "This is the love of God, that we keep his commandments." How could grace be opposed to the love of God? In his book *The Ten Commandments*, Moody says, "I have never seen an honest man who found fault with the Ten Commandments." Another godly man of Moody's type said, "When a man finds fault with the Ten Commandments, you may be sure that one of these commandments is condemning something he is practicing."

Love Upholds the Law

Coming back to Jesus' declaration that the commandments are based on love to God and love to man, and that "on these two commandments hang all the law," we find that, according to Jesus, these two commandments do not dispose of any part of the law, but uphold all the law. The first four commandments define our duty to God, based on love. If a man loves the Lord with all the heart, he will not have other gods, will not bow to images, and will not profane the Lord's name or the Lord's holy day. And if a man loves his neighbor as himself, he will not murder, steal, lie or practice the violation of any of the others of the last six commandments. But the principles of divine love must first be implanted in his heart, because the carnal mind is not subject to the law of God. It would seem from this that a feeling of rebellion against the commandments of God is a sure sign that carnality still dominates the heart.

Since the commandments are spiritual and based on love, they can never fail because "love never faileth." (1 Corinthians 13:8, A.S.V.) Paul further declares, "Love is the fulfilling of the law." Romans 13:10. This statement simply means that love is the carrying out of that which the law embodies by the way of love to God and man. When Cain violated these principles, his wretchedness led him to say, "My punishment is greater than I can bear." Genesis 4:13. It is the purpose of the gospel not to give license to violate these principles, but so to infuse man's heart with love for his fellow men that he will be led to respect these principles This is the love that is "the fulfilling of the law."

As long as human social relations remain, as long as the commandment "Thou shalt love thy neighbor as thyself" is a Christian duty, the last six of the Ten Commandments will remain. The only way to abolish these commandments would be to abolish the social relations between man and man—and then there would be no possibility of violating them.

Man was made with a capacity not only for *social* fellowship with others but also for *spiritual* fellowship with God. The maintenance of this fellowship involved certain principles which, if observed, would ensure its uninterrupted continuity. On the other hand their violation would destroy this fellowship and separate man from God. We need only to refer to what came to our first parents in the Garden of Eden to prove that this is true. We cannot get into the kingdom by good works, but we can shut ourselves out by bad works. To Adam and Eve disobedience (Romans 5:19) proved to be the bad works which shut them out from Eden.

Some modern teachers claim that the Ten Commandments "governed Israel's moral life," and that they came to an end, together with the typical and ceremonial laws which pointed forward to the death of our Lord. It seems unaccountably strange that it will be persistently taught that the moral principles of these commandments neither originated nor applied before Sinai but existed only between then and the cross. Why do not the supporters of this teaching recall that when Cain murdered his brother, he was held under condemnation? Why do they not recall that when Joseph was urged to violate the principle of the seventh commandment, he protested, saying, "How then can I do this great wickedness, and sin against God?" Why can they not understand that it never has been right to have other gods, adore images, and desecrate the Lord's name and day? Why can they not understand that it has never been right to dishonor parents, kill, commit adultery, steal lie, and covet? Why can they not see that Jesus never brought these principles to an end at the cross, or then after a time relegislated nine of them back into force again?

We can illustrate the folly of this argument by supposing that one of a man's ten fingers is giving him trouble, and he wishes to get rid of it. Suppose he goes to a doctor and makes his wishes known. Suppose the physician should argue like this: "The only way I can get rid of the troublesome finger is to cut off all ten and later stick nine of them back on." Sounds foolish, doesn't it? But what about the argument that God abolished all ten of the commandments at the cross to get rid of the "troublesome" Sabbath commandment and then reinstated nine of them later on? This is exactly what the no-Sabbath advocates contend. It does seem that any honest truth seeker could understand that these men are wrong and only trying desperately to get around the truth.

The commandments are enduring principles based on love relations between man and his Maker, and between man and his fellowmen. From the very beginning God never intended that man should have other gods, worship images, or profane the Lord's name or the Sabbath, all of which stand for the recognition of God as Creator. As long as these relationships between God and man last, these principles will exist. The only way to abolish the commandments which unfold these principles would be to abolish the relationships between God and man. Certainly the coming of Jesus into the world never disrupted or destroyed these love relations. How, when "love is the fulfilling of the law," can grace be opposed to love, and love be opposed to grace? Such is not the truth. How can a man preach the love of God with one breath and the abolition of the Ten Commandments with the next? How can such preaching be the truth if love is the fulfilling of the law? Love carries out what it says. Then as long as the commandments remain, the seventh-day Sabbath must remain, since it is one of the commandments of this law of love.

The Decalogue Transcends the "Mosaic System"

We have seen that all the commandments are based on love-relationship principles, and that these relationships between man and God, and between man and man, will endure as long as the world stands. From all this we see that the Ten Commandments are to be considered far more than just a part of the "Mosaic system." If they were merely part of the Mosaic system, then these relationships between man and man, and between man and God, never had any existence before Moses. The scriptures previously cited, however, certainly prove that it was wicked to violate these principles before Moses, and that it is still wicked to violate them since the cross.

It has been said again and again that the standard of righteousness held out in the Ten Commandments was so high man could not reach it, and that, to remedy the situation, Jesus came and did away with the law to lower the standard to something that man could attain. It is true that the Decalogue sets a standard sinful man of himself cannot reach, for human beings are "carnal, sold under sin." (Romans 7:14). But it is not true that the remedy for this inability to keep the law is to do away with the law.

Paul spoke of that defeated life, as far as self-effort was concerned, when he cried out in despair, "O wretched man that I am! who shall deliver me from the body of this death?" Romans 7:24.

"By Us" or "In Us"?

After asking the question, "Who shall deliver me?" Paul gives the answer: "Jesus Christ our Lord." Deliver him from what? From "the law of sin and death" (Romans 8:2)—meaning the "passions of sins" (Romans 7:5, margin) which formerly dominated his life. Did this deliverance give him license to ignore the righteousness of the law, as is the logic of no-lawism? Not so. Let Paul explain. He says that Christ delivered him from the law of carnal impulses in his body so "that the righteousness of the law might be fulfilled in us, who walk not after the flesh, but after the Spirit." (Romans 8:4). Note once more that Paul does not say "*by* us" but "*in* us." The program of "by us" is attaining by works. But "in us" is God "working in you . . . through Jesus." (Hebrews 13:21). That is righteousness by faith.

Note the words "the righteousness of the law." What did Paul mean by the righteousness of the law that is to be fulfilled in us? We know that the term "righteousness of the law: was not the name of some new order of things. It is used so frequently that all surely understand it has reference to that which is demanded by the Ten Commandments. However, we are not left to guess. Romans 9:31,32 states: "But Israel, which followed after the law of righteousness, hath not attained to the law of righteousness. Wherefore? Because they sought it not by faith, but as it were by the works of the law. For they stumbled at that stumblingstone." Of course "that stumblintstone" was Christ. The Israelites tried to attain to "the law of righteousness" without Jesus in their heart; they attempted it by works and failed. This makes it plain that when Paul speaks of the law of righteousness, to which the unbelieving Jews did not attain, he was speaking of the Ten Commandments.

We are now ready for the understanding of Romans 8:1–4, which reads as follows:

"There is therefore now no condemnation to them which are in Christ Jesus, who walk not after the flesh, but after the Spirit. For the law of the Spirit of life in Christ Jesus hath made me free from the law of sin and death. For what the law could not do, in that it was weak through the flesh, God sending his own Son in the likeness of sinful flesh, and for sin, condemned sin in the flesh: that the righteousness of the law might be fulfilled in us, who walk not after the flesh, but after the Spirit."

Now for two important questions: (1) What is the law of sin and death from which, Paul said, Christ had made him free? (2) What is "the righteousness of the law" which is "fulfilled in us"?

Some hold that the law of sin and death means the Ten Commandments, and that Christ had made Paul free from obedience thereto so that he could violate them to accommodate the wicked impulses of the flesh. That would be spiritual anarchy, so we know that is not what he means by being delivered from the law of sin and death.

In Romans 7:25 we find two laws mentioned: "So then with the mind I myself served the law of God; but with the flesh the law of sin." Here we have the law of God and the law of sin. What is the law of sin? Paul tells us in verse twenty-three, where he speaks of "the law of sin which is in my members." The wording proves he is speaking of his fallen nature and the wicked impulses of that nature which, before his conversion, kept him in defeat. Thus we know that when he says in Romans 8:2 that Christ had delivered him from "the law of sin and death," he meant he had been saved from yielding to the impulses of the flesh.

What "the Righteousness of the Law" Includes

Now what is "the righteousness of the law" which is "fulfilled in us"? It is the law of God and the righteousness that it demands, as contrasted with the law of sin. Did the righteousness of the law include Sabbath observance? If not, where is the text which says the law of righteousness, to which Israel did not attain and the Gentiles did, does not include the observance of the seventh day? I have yet to meet the man who has even attempted to prove to me that the righteousness of the law of Romans 8:4 does not include the observance of the seventh day. The fact is, it does, and there is no scriptural escape from that fact. Paul, in Romans 13:9,10 says, "For this, Thou shalt not commit adultery, Thou shalt not kill, Thou shalt not steal, Thou shalt not bear false witness, Thou shalt not covet; and if there be any other commandments, it is briefly comprehended in this saying, namely, Thou shalt love thy neighbor as thyself. Love worketh no ill to his neighbor: therefore love is the fulfilling of the law."

"But," someone will object, "there is not a word in these verses about the seventh day." They mean by this that it was not mentioned and, therefore, is not to be observed. However, there is not a word about the commandment, "Honour thy father and thy mother," or about a number of other commandments. Does that mean such love principles are no longer binding? Certainly not. Paul takes care of the commandments he did not mention by the clause, "If there be any other commandment." This is the same as saying, "There are other commandments which I have not mentioned which are to be included in the statement I am about to make."

Contrasting Israel's rule of life with that of Christians, a certain writer says the Jews had "the law as a rule of life which none were able to keep perfectly."—*Dispensationalism*, p. 423. Defining the Christian's rule of life, the same writer says, "It is to be expected that the injunctions addressed to a perfected heavenly people will be exalted as heaven itself."—*Ibid*., p. 415. Then on page 414 he states: "Almost every intrinsic value contained in the law system is carried forward and incorporated into the present grace system." According to this statement, a large portion of the law system is to be accepted in the Christian's rule of faith. We would suppose, according to this writer's ideas, that about all that was not carried forward of the Ten Commandments was the biblical day of worship.

In that case Christians have nine tenths of the law as their rule of conduct and living. If that is not a logical conclusion, what is?

We would like to inquire, Where is the consistency of claiming that God gave to Israel a rule of life which they could not live up to, and then imposed nine tenths of this same rule of life on Christians?

Power to Obey

To enable Christians to live up to these nine injunctions, this writer further says that "as these requirements are superhuman and yet the doing of them is most essential, God has provided that each individual thus saved shall be indwelt by the Holy Spirit to the end that he may, by dependence on the Spirit and by the power of the Spirit, live a supernatural, God-honoring life—not, indeed, to be accepted, but because he *is* accepted."—*Ibid.*, p. 415. That is exactly what we are teaching; however we claim that the divine arrangement is made for obedience to all the Ten Commandments instead of "almost" all. It is a strange teaching that contends that through the power of the Spirit a Christian can obey almost all the law, but that for the same Spirit to enable a Christian to obey "all" is asking too much for that Power to do! If it takes that sort of reasoning to get rid of the observance of the Sabbath day, it must indeed be difficult to remove!

The Spirit-instructed people of God in the Old Testament never felt or taught that man, left to himself, could do the will of God. We read in Jeremiah 10:23: "O Lord, I know that the way of man is not in himself; it is not in man that walketh to direct his steps." Can we find anywhere in the New Testament a teaching stronger than this: that without divine help man cannot live up to God's rule of life? Let us take another verse: "Can the Ethiopian change his skin, or the leopard his spots? then may ye also do good, that are accustomed to do evil." Jeremiah 13:23. Here we find, as in the New Testament, that the doing of God's will without His help is the most impossible thing that can be thought of. The provisions of the Old Testament was this: "Let him trust in the name of the Lord, and stay upon his God." Isaiah 50:10. The injunction was as follows: "Let Israel hope in the Lord: for with the Lord there is mercy, and with him is plenteous redemption." Psalm 130:7. Scores of scriptures of the same import could be cited. But what has been quoted certainly proves that the same divine help that is offered in the New Testament was not withheld from the people of the Old Testament. The idea that God is no respecter of persons is taught all through the Bible.

"By Grace . . . Through Faith"

It has been rightly contended by some who would do away with the Decalogue that obedience is not rendered by the New Testament Christian "to be accepted, but because he is accepted." The same was true in Old Testament times, however. David prayed, "Save me, and I shall keep thy testimonies." Psalm 119:146. Here, just as in the New Testament, man was saved, and then obedience followed as the fruits.

At one time I heard a Bible teacher commenting on the book of Ephesians. When she came to "For by grace are ye saved through faith; and that not of yourselves: it is the gift of God: not of works, lest any man should boast" (Ephesians 2:8,9), she took occasion to denounce the Ten Commandments with great bitterness. She declared that those who taught that they should be kept now were false teachers of the worst sort, and were putting folks back under the old Mosaic system.

As the teacher went on, of course, she finally reached chapter six, verses two and three, which read, "Honour thy father and mother; which is the first commandment with promise; that it may be well with thee, and that thou mayest live long on the earth." I thought, Look out, teacher! You are having Paul put us under the law again! Your comments on grace in the second chapter demolished every one of the Ten Commandments, and here in the sixth chapter you are reading from Paul that if the fifth command were obeyed, great favors would follow.

The truth is this: What both the Old and the New Testament designate as obedience some modern teachers brand as salvation by works. Certainly Paul did not hold to that error. He made it plain that we are saved by grace, but that at the same time the Ten Commandments should be kept. The expression "saved by grace" does not mean saved *to* sin but saved *from* sin; and "sin," says God's Word, "is the transgression of the law." 1 John 3:4. So the doctrine of being saved by grace does not give license to dishonor parents or to violate any of the other commandments. It makes provision for obedience through the power of the indwelling Spirit. In fact, 1 John 2:4 states, "He that saith, I know him, and keepeth not his commandments, is a liar, and the truth is not in him." 1 John 2:4.

As is well known, the dispensationalists represent what is often termed the fundamentalist wing of Protestantism. They have separated themselves from the modernists, who, they claim, hold to the theory of organic evolution and deny the miracles of the New Testament, the virgin birth, the bodily resurrection of Christ, and supernaturalism in general. The fundamentalists can very readily show that these teachings are a far-flung departure from those of Wesley, Barnes, Moody, and others of similar sound faith. However, the tragic thing is that these same fundamentalists have departed from the Bible and the sound teachings of Wesley, Moody, Barnes, and Clarke by embracing errors equally as dangerous to moral and spiritual life as those of the modernists. We refer especially to the contention that God's holy law was abrogated at the cross. Let us see what John Wesley has to say concerning that deadly error. In his *Sermons on Several Occasions*, volume one, he says:

"But the moral law contained in the Ten Commandments, and enforced by the prophets, He [Jesus] did not take away. It was not the design of His coming to revoke any part of this. This is a law which can never be broken, which 'stands fast as the faithful witness in heaven.' The moral law stands on an entirely different foundation from the ceremonial or ritual law. . . . Every part of this law must remain in force upon all mankind and in all ages."

Moody says, "The people must be made to understand that the Ten Commandments are still binding, and there is a penalty attached to their violation."—*Weighed and Wanting*, p. 16.

In his *Notes on the Epistle to the Romans*, commenting on Romans 3:31 (which says: "Do we then make void the law through faith? God forbid: yea, we establish the law"), Albert Barnes writes:

"*Do we then make void the law*? Do we render it vain and useless; do we destroy its moral obligation; do we prevent obedience to it by the doctrine of justification by faith? This was an *objection* which would naturally be made, and which has thousands of times been since made. . . . The word *law* here, I understand as referring to the *moral law*, and not merely to the Old Testament. . . . This [text] is an explicit denial of any such tendency. *Yea, we establish the law*. That is, by the doctrine of justification by faith . . . the moral law is confirmed, its obligation is enforced, obedience to it is secured."—pp. 103,104.

If these expositors of God's Holy Word were living today, they would surely class the teachings of dispensationalism relative to the abolition of the Ten Commandments with the deadly errors of modernism.

Chapter 4
Dispensationalism

The claims made by the dispensational school of Bible interpretation, if carried to a logical conclusion, would charge God with despotic injustice and partiality. Dispensationalists hold that the era from Moses to Christ must be designated as the dispensation of the law. They teach that during this time God placed man on an exclusive "merit system" of salvation by works, and that the "saved by grace" system was not introduced until after the cross.

A spokesman for this theory contends that "under the Mosaic law, the individual Israelite . . . was on an unyielding meritorious basis."—*Bibliotheca Sacra*, Vol. 3, p. 440. Even a novice in the knowledge of the Scriptures can understand that man has never been able to do anything to atone for his sins and effect his pardon and justification, thus working himself into acceptance with God so that He would owe him eternal life.

The Jews were warned over and over of the futility of attempting to gain salvation by works and were held accountable for even trying it. "But Israel, which followed after the law of righteousness, hath not attained to the law of righteousness. Wherefore? Because they sought it not by faith, but as it were by the works of the law." Romans 9:32, 32. The Holy Spirit condemned their seeking righteousness by works rather than by faith, proving that from Moses to Christ it was their privilege to obtain righteousness by faith.

What becomes of the claim that God put them on a merit system of works? It is made groundless. David prayed, "Save me, and I shall keep thy testimonies." Psalm 119:146. If God had put him exclusively on the merit system of salvation, he would have prayed, "I will keep Thy testimonies *in order* to merit salvation." But David said salvation must come *before* commandment keeping. He also stated, "Thou desirest not sacrifice; else would I give it: thou delightest not in burnt offering. The sacrifices of God are a broken spirit and a contrite heart, O God, thou wilt not despise." Psalm 51:16,17. If this is not saved-by-grace doctrine, if this is not God doing the works for man instead of man doing the works of God, how else could this language be explained? Surely it cannot support the teaching that in the days of David man was put on an exclusive merit system to obtain salvation!

Jeremiah 13:23, speaking of the impossibility of man saving himself, says, "Can the Ethiopian change his skin, or the leopard his spots? then may ye also do good, that are accustomed to do evil." If God had put Jeremiah on a merit system, we see from this text that He repudiated it as an utter impossibility. It is not true that God put man on a regime of works until Christ came and then changed it to grace. This is not what John meant when he said, "The law was given by Moses, but grace and truth came by Jesus Christ." John 1:17. The Jews were trying to attain to the righteousness of the law apart from union with Christ. Christ came to turn them from failure to Himself. He said, "Without me ye can do nothing." In receiving Him, they received grace and truth.

Obedience Versus Legalism

The dispensationalists confuse obedience with legalism and works. They read where God told the Israelites that if they would obey Him, He would undertake for them in many ways; but if they were disobedient, they would thereby forfeit these blessings. This, claim the dispensationalists, is the merit system. We would like to inquire about the meaning of Hebrews 5:9, which declares, "And being made perfect, he became the author of eternal salvation unto all them that obey him." If this came from the Old Testament, instead of from the New, it would be contended that it puts eternal salvation on the merit system of works, and that salvation would be forfeited if obedience were not forthcoming. But since this verse is in the New Testament, we will leave the dispensationalists to wrestle with it. What they term "works," the Bible calls "obedience."

Then what about Acts 5:32? It reads, "And we are his witnesses of these things, and so is also the Holy Ghost, whom God hath given to them that obey him." Will this be called the merit system because the promise is to the obedient?

There are Old Testament texts very similar to the New Testament just quoted. Deuteronomy 6:17,18 reads: "Ye shall diligently keep the commandments of the Lord your God . . . that it may be well with thee, and that thou mayest go in and possess the good land." It will be contended that the going into the good land was dependent upon obedience, and that disobedience would keep the Israelites out. What is the difference between this condition (if we wish to call it that) and the one mentioned in Revelation 22:14: "Blessed are they that do his commandments, that they may have right to the tree of life, and may enter in through the gates into the city"? Deuteronomy 6:17,18 states, "Keep the commandments" and "go in"; and Revelation 22:14 in the New Testament says, "Do his commandments" and "enter in." Where is the difference? We will leave it with those who are fearful and afraid of the word "obey," lest it get them into works and take them away from grace.

The Law Before Sinai

The Scriptures teach that both law and grace have existed since Adam sinned—the law to define and condemn sin, and grace to convert and save from sin. The Bible says that "all have sinned," and that "sin is not imputed when there is no law." Romans 3:23; 5:13. These texts prove that sin has always been associated with transgression of the law, and that it has always been impossible for one to exist without the other.

Two verses are often quoted (and both are greatly misunderstood) to prove that the law of God had no existence before Sinai. These verses are Romans 5:20 and Romans 5:13. "Moreover the law entered, that the offense might abound. But where sin abounded, grace did much more abound." "For until the law sin was in the world, but sin is not imputed when there is no law."

The two confusing expressions in these verses are "the law entered" and "until the law." It is contended that these phrases mean that between Adam and Sinai the law had no existence. But that this is not the meaning is easily discovered by the statement that "sin is not imputed when there is no law." Since sin was imputed to Cain when he slew his brother, and would have been imputed to Joseph had he violated the seventh commandment, certainly there was a law which prohibited murder and adultery. In fact, some weeks before the law was proclaimed on Sinai, the Lord told Moses that He would prove whether the people would walk in His law or not. (Exodus 16:4) The test had reference to the observance of the Sabbath. The record says: "And it came to pass, that there went out some of the people on the seventh day for to gather, and they found none. And the Lord said unto Moses, How long refuse ye to keep my commandments and my laws?" Exodus 16:27,28.

This text proves that what God called His law existed before Sinai, and that this law enjoined the observance of the seventh day. It also makes plain that the expressions "until the law" and "the law entered" cannot mean that the law had no existence before it was spoken by the Lord at Sinai. These statements simply mean that the law had not existed in written form. The children of Israel had largely lost sight of the principles of love to God and love to man while in Egypt, and the law entered in written form that the law might abound. (Romans 5:20). When they heard these commandments spoken by the mouth of God, and knew that they were written with the finger of God (Exodus 31:18) so they would not forget them, they had it brought more forcibly to their attention that some of the things they were practicing were sinful and a violation of God's law. This is what is meant by the statement "that the offence might abound."

It has been contended that since Nehemiah 9:13,14 says, "Thou camest down also upon mount Sinai . . . and madest known unto them thy holy sabbath," the law, and especially the holy Sabbath, had no existence previous to this time. But what about Ezekiel 20:5? This text reads: "I chose Israel, and lifted up mine hand unto the seed of the house of Jacob, and made myself known unto them in the land of Egypt, when I lifted up mine hand unto them, saying, I am the Lord your God." The Lord said He made Himself known unto them. Does this mean that the Lord had no existence until that time? Certainly not. And if this does not mean that the Lord had no existence until then, why should it be thought that the law and the Sabbath had no existence before Sinai simply because Nehemiah said, "Thou . . . madest known unto them thy holy sabbath"?

Both God and the holy Sabbath existed before Sinai, but Israel had largely lost sight of the true God and the true Sabbath while in Egypt. This is evidenced by their worshiping the golden calf, saying, "These be thy gods, O Israel, which brought the up out of the land of Egypt" (Exodus 32:4), and by the fact that, after they were instructed not to gather manna on the seventh day, "there went out some of the people on the seventh day for to gather, and found none." It was then that the Lord said, "How long refuse ye to keep my commandments and my laws?" All of which proves that the law existed (uncodified) before Sinai. Therefore, because the people had largely lost sight of the principles contained therein, the law was given them in written form, and the expression "until the law" simply means until it was spoken on Mount Sinai.

"Not Under the Law"

Paul says to those newly converted to Christ, "For sin shall not have dominion over you: for ye are not under the law, but under grace." Romans 6:14. There are those who put a dispensational interpretation on this text, although the context makes such an application impossible. He was writing to those who had been baptized and had risen to "walk in newness of life" (Romans 6:4), to those who had become "dead to sin" (verse 2) and were not to "live any longer therein." Before this change had come into their lives, they were "under [the condemnation of] the law." But having accepted by faith the substitutionary death of Christ, which paid the penalty of the violated law, they were no longer under judicial condemnation of the law, but under grace. The phrase "under the law" as here used is explained in Romans 3:19 as meaning "guilty before God": "Now we know that what things soever the law saith, it saith to them who are under the law: that every mouth may be stopped, and all the world may become guilty before God."

This text states that all the world is under the law, which is just another way of saying that "all have sinned," and because of this "judgment came upon all men to condemnation." (Romans 5:18). So then "under the law" as here used means "guilty before God." The Apostle Paul, in writing to those at Rome who were justified by faith, tells them that on account of this faith transaction they are no longer under the law—that is, under its judicial condemnation—but under grace. (Romans 6:14). The next verse makes it very plain that the Holy Spirit foresaw that some would seize upon this statement to teach that "not under the law" means "not under any obligation to obey the commandments of God," and "free to violate them without condemnation." The verse reads, "What then? shall we sin, because we are not under the law, but under grace? God forbid." Romans 6:15.

Those who put a dispensational interpretation upon the statement, "Ye are not under the law, but under grace," contend that the old dispensation (before the cross) is to be spoken of as "under the law" and that the new dispensation (after the cross) is to be spoken of as "under grace." The reasoning of such teaching is that before Christ people were to respect and obey the commandments of God, and this is what "under the law" means, but that since Christ came, the commandments may be ignored and disobeyed, and that is what "under grace" means.

Many popular preachers try to get around the observance of the Lord's holy day by saying, "We are not under the law but under grace." What they mean is that before the cross men were under obligation to be obedient, but that since then they are under grace and free to desecrate the Sabbath day. Why do they not put that same construction on the other commandments of the Decalogue? Why could not the thief, the liar, the murderer, and the adulterer just as logically justify their practices by saying, "I am not under the law"?

The claim that before the cross it was all law and no grace, and that since the cross it is all grace and no law, is unscriptural. Speaking of Moses' times, the Bible says, "Moreover the law entered [in written form], that the offence might abound. But where sin abounded, grace did much more abound." Romans 5:20.

Of prime importance are the words "Grace did much more abound." Apparently in the old dispensation, before the cross, abounding grace was provided to save man from the transgression of the law. Nothing could be further from the truth than to teach that in the days of Moses or Abraham God placed man on a regime of justification by works of the law, and shut him off from all access to the grace of God. Never! The statement, "By the deeds of the law there shall no flesh be justified," was just as true then as today. Since all have sinned, the law could not witness that they were innocent, even as it cannot do that for transgressors in this age. Further combating the idea that any man has ever been justified by works, the Apostle Paul brings up the case of Abraham and says: "What shall we say then that Abraham our father, as pertaining to the flesh, hath found? For if Abraham were justified by works, he hath whereof to glory; but not before God." Romans 4:1,2.

The remainder of the chapter deals with Abraham's faith as the reason for his justification. In verse sixteen Paul says, "Therefore it [justification] is of faith, that it might be by grace"; and this was with reference to Abraham. Abraham's case agrees with Romans 5:1: "Therefore being justified by faith, we have peace with God through our Lord Jesus Christ." We find also that in the days of Abraham, just as now, being justified by faith did not mean rebellion against the precepts of God. Although Abraham was justified by faith, God says, "Abraham obeyed my voice, and kept my charge, my commandments, my statutes, and my laws." Genesis 26:5.

"Dispensation of Grace"

In the light of Paul's statement about Abraham's justification, what becomes of the claim, so often heard, that the age before the cross is to be known as the "dispensation of the law" and the age since the cross as the "dispensation of grace"? This claim is unsupportable when we again recall that Paul declared, "Where sin abounded, grace did much more abound." Romans 5:20. And Jeremiah 31:2 says, "The people . . . found grace in the wilderness; even Israel, when I went to cause him to rest."

Turning to Hebrews 11, we find the expressions "by faith" and "through faith" more than twenty times. This chapter begins with Abel and comes right down to a few centuries before Christ. How confusing, therefore, and how unscriptural to teach that in the old dispensation God's plan for saving men was "by the works of the law," but later, at the cross, God abolished the Ten Commandments and changes His plan!

Those who teach this doctrine, practically without exception, try to dispense with the fourth commandment. When the matter of keeping the seventh-day Sabbath is mentioned, they immediately evade the question by saying, "We are now living in the dispensation of grace." But should one inquire whether Christians may violate the commandment prohibiting the profaning of the Lord's name, he will certainly not receive the same answer. One will not be told, "Well, that was when people were under the law, but now we are under grace, and that commandment is no longer to be respected." Yet when the command that man should not "profane the sabbath day" (Nehemiah 13:17) is brought up, the answer is entirely different. Go through the commandments except the fourth, and not once will the "not under the law" argument, to evade obedience to these principles, be resorted to. But when one asks whether man should "profane the sabbath day," then he will immediately hear the 'under grace" argument. Therefore, in the final analysis the one objective above every other for calling the time before Christ as the "dispensation of law" and the time since Christ as the "dispensation of grace" is to excuse Sabbath desecration. The inconsistency of this argument is discovered when it is applied to the other nine commandments of the same law.

From Adam until the present time God's plan of saving men has been the same. Sin has always involved man in a relationship of condemnation that left him powerless of himself to step into a relationship of justification with God. The "how" of this change of relationships with reference to condemnation and justification has always been the same. It has never been of works, but always "by grace . . . through faith."

Dangers of Dispensationalism

The dispensationalists distort the doctrine of "saved by grace" to the extent of claiming that disobedience will not in the least bring about a forfeiture of their standing of justification with God. A writer in *Bibliotheca Sacra*, Volume 93, page 416, says this justification-by-faith doctrine of the New Testament also provides for "an absolute security from all condemnation" in the future. They teach that no matter what the nature of the disobedience may be, they can never come under the condemnation of the law. They further teach that if an "out of Christ" man steals, God holds him under the condemnation; but if a dispensationalist steals, God does not condemn him for it. He is supposed to have "license," but the open sinner is held accountable.

This is upholding, in principle, the Roman Catholic dogma of indulgence. For, according to the "security" argument, if faith-justified men willfully commit sin or practice sin, this does not interfere with their justified standing. Of course it means, too, that they need never again confess their sins to God. That would not be necessary in the least, for—sin or no sin—they are absolutely immune to condemnation. Anyone can readily see the danger of such a doctrine. It leads men to depend upon a past "justification act" of God for salvation, rather than a continual trust in Christ. In fact if this theory were true, men would have no need of Christ for salvation after justification. Their salvation, they are taught, is secure, and they (logically) no longer require a mediator for sin between themselves and God. By one act God removed the necessity of a daily Saviour, for "they are forgiven all trespasses to such a degree that they will never come into condemnation."—*Ibid.*, p. 412.

A proponent of dispensationalism says that Christians "are forgiven all trespasses to such a degree that they will never come into condemnation"; and he contends that they enjoy "an absolute security from condemnation" because they are positionally "in Christ Jesus," and that sin or disobedience cannot disrupt this position.

Thus if they can never again come into condemnation, they never again need Christ. They can say, "Jesus, I have been justified and am 'secure,' and from now on I will trust in something which happened back yonder at a revival; I will trust in a past act, which sin cannot undo, rather than maintain daily fellowship with a Person to keep me from falling away and being lost." Such a fallacy about salvation is an extremely dangerous error, because it does away completely with the necessity of continuing to trust in Christ for salvation even after one has been justified. According to such a teaching, the transaction that brings salvation has been made, Jesus can go His way, and it is no longer necessary to look to Him in faith. This is the no-law philosophy of salvation, which has just as little room for Christ as for His law.

An example of this is the case of a clergyman who killed a man and the following Sunday preached from the text, "There is therefore now no condemnation to them which are in Christ Jesus." Romans 8:1. The inference was that since he was in Christ, there could be to him no condemnation for the violation of the commandment, "Thou shalt not kill." No wonder such people also hold that violation of the Sabbath commandment means nothing! Such a perverted interpretation of grace!

The dangerous extremes to which this doctrine is carried are almost unbelievable. It actually holds that God puts a premium upon willful sin, to the degree that one who persists in sin will get to heaven all the sooner. One of the most popular national radio evangelists once declared that the drunkards of 1 Corinthians continued in sin until God had "to take them home," and that He did this because the chastisement which He laid upon them failed to stop them from getting drunk. We have only to turn to chapter six, verses nine and ten of the same epistle to find that Paul positively declares that drunkards "shall not inherit the kingdom of God."

The advocates of dispensationalism hold that those practicing the vilest form of adultery are incapable of being lost. They cite 1 Corinthians 5:1 as proof: "It is reported commonly that there is fornication among you, and such fornication as is not so much as named among the Gentiles, that one should have his father's wife." Then they quote verse five, which states that the church was to "deliver such an one unto Satan for the destruction of the flesh, that the spirit might be saved."

This text does not say *will* be saved, but *may* be saved. There is a much better chance of "such an one" being saved if he is excommunicated in order to teach him the sinfulness of his sin than if he is retained in the church and told that if he does not give up his sin, God will kill him and "take him to heaven."

This latter doctrine boldly proclaims to millions of the vilest sinners that if at some time in the past they have been accepted by God, then never in the future is it possible for them to sin *away* that relationship. It is taught that God will chastise them for a season, but if they continue to sin, no matter how vile or how often repeated, He will eventually cause them to die and "go home to be with the Lord." This, they claim, is what it means to be "saved by grace."

Warnings

Anyone believing this false "under grace" teaching might well read prayerfully the following scriptures:

"Know ye not that the unrighteous shall not inherit the kingdom of God" Be not deceived: neither fornicators, nor idolaters, nor adulterers . . . nor thieves, nor covetous, nor drunkards . . . shall inherit the kingdom of God." 1 Corinthians 6:9,10.

"But the fearful, and unbelieving, and the abominable, and murderers, and whoremongers, and sorcerers, and idolaters, and all liars, shall have their part in the lake which burneth with fire and brimstone: which is the second death." Revelation 21:8.

Such teaching is, as one version translates Jude 4, turning "the grace of our God into immorality." Let us remember that Jesus came to save His people *from* their sins and not *in* their sins, and that the book of Revelation repeats again and again that it is only the overcomer who will be saved.

As long as men are in Christ Jesus, they are in fellowship with God. But the Bible denies the claim that sin-practicing cannot disrupt or sever this "in Christ Jesus" state. In John 15:2 Jesus says, "Every branch in me that beareth not fruit he taketh away." To prevent this, the injunction is, "Abide in me." The verb "abide" denotes *active* faith. Then Jesus adds, "If a man abide not in me, he is cast forth as a branch, and is withered; and men gather them and cast them into the fire, and they are burned," verse 6. So if man does not continue this active faith in Christ, he thereby, according to Jesus, destroys the "in me" relationship and is severed, and in the end he is burned. Luke 8:13 states, "They on the rock are they, which, when they hear, receive the word with joy; and these have no root, which for a while believe, and in time of temptation fall away." It is clear that if these individuals had continued to believe, they would not have fallen away. Let it be noted that during the time they were believing, they were not in a fallen-away state. But active faith did not continue, and as a result they did fall away.

This proves that justification comes and is maintained by faith. It does not come by works, and neither is it maintained by works. But the fruit will be the works of righteousness, for "faith without works is dead" (James 2:26); and "he that saith, I know him, and keepeth not his commandments, is a liar, and the truth is not in him." 1 John 2:4. A justified man cannot go into a state of lawlessness and spiritual anarchy and at the same time not come again under condemnation. (1 Corinthians 6:9,10).

Let us state this unscriptural teaching like this:

I'm "saved by grace," oh, happy condition!
I can transgress every day and still claim remission.
Nothing in the law has any claim on me,
For being "under grace," I'm entirely free.
I can have other gods as often as I please,
And have a good conscience—entirely at ease.
Images of all kinds I can worship and adore,
Since I'm "free from the law"—not bound any more.
I can remain "under grace" until the day I die,
Even though God's name I profane and deny.
"Remember the Sabbath day" was not for me or you;
That was "under the law" and only for the Jew.
My father and mother I need not respect;
That's for those who God's grace reject.
I can kill, despise, and everybody hate,
And still have a welcome at the pearly gate.
And concerning adultery heard from Sinai's mount,
I can break every word and not render an account.
And since it is "by grace" before the Lord I kneel,
I am free to rob, plunder, and steal.
And if about my neighbor I should daily lie,
I'll not even face that in the great by-and-by.
I can covet my neighbor's goods—even his wife—
And stay "saved by grace" every day of my life.
So let's all beware of that Sabbatarian creed:
That it's "grace" producing "obedience" that all of us need!

Chapter 5

The Eternal Seventh-day Sabbath

There is one fact we must not forget as we examine the strange arguments against the law of God: that they are put forth in order to destroy the memorial of our Creator established to commemorate His holy day of rest.

The fact that our Creator rested on the seventh day cannot be dismissed as something that was done without any reason, even as Jesus did not institute and observe the Lord's Supper without a reason. Jesus intended to show something: "As often as ye eat this bread, and drink this cup, ye do shew the Lord's death till he come." 1 Corinthians 11:26. Using this text as an illustration, we see that the Scriptures teach that the Lord "rested on the seventh day" and also made out of this day a spiritual institution to show something. That something must be very important, since it was to be shown so frequently—every seventh day. What is it that the observance of the Sabbath shows? The answer is plainly implied in the fourth commandment: "Remember the sabbath day, to keep it holy. . . . For in six days the Lord made heaven and earth, the sea, and all that in them is, and rested on the seventh day: wherefore the Lord blessed the sabbath day, and hallowed it." Exodus 20:8,11. Here the reason for keeping the seventh day is stated. The reason is a truth that is as immutable as God; it is something that can never be rendered untrue or repudiated. That reason is the *recognition of God as Creator*.

There will never come a time when it will be right to ignore God as the Creator. The commandment says, "Wherefore the Lord blessed the sabbath day." The word "wherefore" means "on account of the reason just stated." The reason just stated before the word "wherefore" is: "For in six days the Lord made heaven and earth, the sea, and all that in them is, and rested the seventh day." God asks us to rest on the seventh day to show that we believe that He made heaven and earth. The recognition of God as the Creator of all things is a truth so fundamental to salvation that to repudiate it means damnation. As long as the truth which the observance of the seventh day sets forth is to be recognized, just so long will the observance of the Sabbath be in force. The coming of Jesus to the earth did not do away with the necessity of man's recognizing God as the Creator.

Sabbath Observance Honors the Creator

The observance of the seventh day is a repudiation of evolution. It would be absurd for a man who does not believe in the atonement to observe the Lord's Supper. It would be just as absurd for a man to observe the Sabbath who denies that God created the world. The observance of the Sabbath sets forth the observer's belief that God did create the world according to the claims stated in the Sabbath commandment. The importance of the observance of the Sabbath is more clearly and forcibly understood as we continue to search the Scriptures and find that the fact of God's ability to create, as opposed to the inability of other gods to create, is the distinguishing attribute of the true God.

In the following scriptures the true God is contrasted with the false gods by virtue of the fact that He has creative power and the others do not: "For all the gods of the nations are idols: but the Lord made the heavens." Psalm 96:5. "But the Lord is the true God. . . . Thus shall ye say unto them, The gods that have not made the heavens and the earth, even they shall perish. . . . He hath made the earth by his power." Jeremiah 10:10–12.

It will be noted that in the introduction of the true God, as contrasted with other gods, the prophet says, "He hath made the earth." In speaking of the false gods, he says they "have not made the heavens and the earth." The power to create is what marks the true God from the other gods.

When Jonah was introducing the God he worshiped, he said to those on the ship who worshiped other gods: "I am an Hebrew; and I fear the Lord, the God of heaven, which hath made the sea and the dry land." Jonah 1:9.

All through the Old Testament the true God is thus distinguished. It is the same in the New Testament. In Acts 4:24 the disciples prayed, "Lord, thou art God, which has made heaven and earth, and the sea, and all that in them is."

These words are from the Sabbath commandment, which says, "The Lord made heaven and earth, the sea, and all that in them is." The disciples were praying to the Lord whose creative power is acknowledged in the observance of the memorial of creation. He is the true God.

In making known to the people of Lystra the true God, Paul said, "We . . . preach unto you that ye should turn from these vanities unto the living God, which made heaven and earth, and the sea, and all things that are therein." Acts 14:15.

Here again we find the disciples quoting from the Sabbath commandment.

While Paul waited at Athens, "his spirit was stirred in him, when he saw the city wholly given to idolatry." In introducing the people to the true God, he said, "For as I passed by, and beheld your devotions, I found an altar with this inscription, TO THE UNKNOWN GOD. Whom therefore ye ignorantly worship, him declare I unto you. God that made the world and all things therein, seeing that he is Lord of heaven and earth." Acts 17:16, 23, 24. In declaring the true God to those philosophers, Paul introduced Him as the One "that made the world," and then said, "He is Lord."

The judgment-hour message that is being proclaimed to every nation, and kindred, and tongue, and people today calls upon them to "worship him that made heaven, and earth, and the sea, and the fountains of waters." Revelation 14:7.

This array of scriptural references should convince anyone that the great truth which God intended should be perpetuated by the observance of the Sabbath is that the one and only true God is the Creator. By our observance of the Sabbath we show that we repudiate evolution and accept the Genesis account of creation, acknowledging God as the Creator. As long as it is in man's duty to recognize God as the Creator, the Sabbath will endure.

In Psalm 111:4 we are told that God "made his wonderful works to be remembered." The reason is that His works remind us of creation, and creation reminds us of the Creator, and the Creator is the only true God. Since He "hath made his wonderful works to be remembered," it would be only natural that, at the close of the week in which these wonderful works were done, He should institute a memorial by which we would be reminded from week to week of them. Thus we would never forget who is the true God, and drift into idolatry, or deny Him as the Creator by accepting the theory of evolution. So at the close of creation week, on the seventh day, the Creator rested from all His works; and at the same time He "blessed the seventh day, and sanctified it." (Genesis 2:1–3). That the seventh day was sanctified as a memorial is proved by the fact that the first word in the Sabbath commandment is "remember." Remember what? "Remember the sabbath day, to keep it holy." What for? "For in six days the Lord made heaven and earth." The Sabbath is a memorial of His wonderful works which He "hath made . . . to be remembered."

The theory of evolution denies the great truth for which the observance of the seventh day stands. In this generation, when this theory is so widespread, how divinely planned it is that the Sabbath truth should be especially emphasized that all may see its meaning and begin observing it!

In the face of these facts, how can it be intelligently and scripturally claimed that this creation memorial is Jewish in origin or application? Actually the Creator rested on the seventh day more than two thousand years before there were any Jews.

Was it a matter of indifference with God as to whether or not man from Adam to Moses recognized Him as the Creator? Then was his recognition to cease at the cross? The claim is that everything about the law system of the Old Testament came to an end at the cross, and yet dispensationalists claim that "almost every intrinsic value contained in the law system is carried forward and incorporated into the present grace system." Since all the fundamentalist adherents of this school are so against the observance of the creation Sabbath, they must feel that its existence had no particular importance and, therefore, was not brought forward. In fact they condemn the observance of the Sabbath day just as vehemently as they would the practice of lying or immorality. They hold that it had no essential value whatever.

Opposers of the seventh-day Sabbath claim that although God made the Sabbath for man, it had no real value to him, physically or spiritually. They claim that man could have gotten along without it just as well; and since that was the case, it came to an end at the cross. It seems strange indeed that God would say so much in favor of the observance of the Sabbath, even to meting out the death sentence to those who presumptuously violated it, if it had no intrinsic value whatever. It is not pleasant to show up such absurd inconsistencies, but at times it is necessary to show how very groundless are the claims of those who despise the Creator's rest day.

The Blessings of the Sabbath

Since the law is spiritual, there is no escaping the fact that the holy Sabbath is a spiritual institution. It was a day of "holy convocation." (Leviticus 23:3). The joyful quality of the day is expressed by David in Psalm 42:4; "When I remember these things, I pour out my soul in me: for I had gone with the multitude, I went with them to the house of God, with the voice of joy and praise, with a multitude that kept holyday." The fact that the Sabbath was to be devoted entirely to the Lord, the fact that it was to be spent as a day of joy and praise, proves that the provisions of the fourth commandment contributed more toward making man spiritual than any other commandment of the ten. To deprive man of the spiritual advantages of the Sabbath, the enemy has always sought to lead man to profane the Sabbath day. "What evil thing is this that ye do, and profane the sabbath day?" Nehemiah 13:17. To profane the Sabbath day was, in the eyes of the Lord, an evil thing.

The thought that the Sabbath is a spiritual institution is beautifully brought out in Isaiah 58:13,14: "If thou turn away thy foot from the sabbath, from doing thy pleasure on my holy day; and call the sabbath a delight, the holy of the Lord, honourable; and shalt honour him, not doing thine own ways, nor finding thine own pleasure, nor speaking thine own words: then shalt thou delight thyself in the Lord." The Sabbath was always to be a refreshing time when men were in a special sense to delight themselves in the Lord.

A verse found in Acts will explain the spiritual advantages the Lord intended the Sabbath to bring to those who in spirit observe it: "On the sabbath we went out of the city by a river side, where prayer was wont to be made; and we sat down, and spake unto the women which resorted thither." Acts 16:13.

We see from this statement that, just as in Old Testament times, so also in the days of the Apostle Paul, the Sabbath was a day of gathering for prayer and worship. Supporting this thought, we read that "the Gentiles besought that these words might be preached to them the next sabbath." Paul agreed to this, "and the next sabbath day came almost the whole city together to hear the word of God." (Acts 13:42–44). Thus we find that, in apostolic times, the Sabbath was looked upon as the day for coming together "to hear the word of God."

The Sabbath is the Lord's appointed day for laying aside all thoughts and activities of a secular nature and for coming together to hear the Word of God. So when Paul said, "The law is spiritual," he included the institution of the Sabbath, which was to be devoted exclusively to things that are spiritual. We inquire: Was that gathering when almost the whole city came together to hear the Word of God of "intrinsic value" to those who were present? We find here—and there is no escaping the fact—that the same use was made of the Sabbath in New Testament times as in the days of the ancient prophets. The New Testament references are as clear and plain as those which we have cited from the Old. The institution and its purpose continued. It was not Sabbath rest, but man-made regulations as to how it should be kept, that was the yoke of bondage.

To the uninformed, certain attacks on the Sabbath day tend to breed a feeling of contempt and disregard for it, and that is just what Satan wishes. But it is the Lord's will that we call the Sabbath a delight. The word "delight" as here used suggests something that brings spiritual joy and happiness. This being the case, how it must displease the Lord of the Sabbath day to hear it belittled, denounced, and set at nought!

Sabbath a Sign of What to Whom?

It will be said over and over again by opponents of the true Lord's day that "the Sabbath was a sign between God and the children of Israel"; and then they use this statement to frame some farfetched and unscriptural argument as to why Gentiles should not observe it. These opponents make no effort to give the Bible information concerning the fact that the Sabbath really was, and is, a sign. The Bible makes plain in what sense it is a sign, and when we discover this, it will prove how impossible it would be for the Sabbath ever to be changed or done away with.

Those looking for the truth on this particular aspect of the Sabbath question should note the following:

"Speak thou also unto the children of Israel, saying, Verily, my sabbaths ye shall keep: for it is a sign between me and you . . . that ye may know that I am the Lord that doth sanctify you. . . . It is a sign between me and the children of Israel for ever: for in six days the Lord made heaven and earth, and on the seventh day he rested, and was refreshed." Exodus 31:13, 17.

These verses explain in what sense and for what reason the Sabbath was a sign. Its observance was a sign that men recognized that the One they worshiped was the Lord. To quote again, "That ye may know that I am the Lord." What had the Lord, whom they worshiped, done which proved that He was the true God, as contrasted with the gods of the heathen nations about them? The answer is this: "For in six days the Lord made heaven and earth." Exodus 31:17. The other gods did not make heaven and earth. But the fact that the children of Israel observed the Sabbath was the sign that they believed the God whom they worshiped was the creator, and that they repudiated the gods of the nations about them. David puts it this way: "For all the gods of the nations are idols: but the Lord made the heavens." Psalm 96:5.

So we see that the observance of the Sabbath on the part of the children of Israel was a sign of their recognition of the Lord as the true God. Thus the Sabbath is a sign of the most fundamental truth of the universe, namely that there is only one true God and creator.

Ezekiel 20:20 states: "Hallow my sabbaths; and they shall be a sign between me and you, that ye may know that I am the Lord your God."

This statement is true because the One who made the heavens and the earth is the true God; and at the close of His creative work He established a memorial to be observed as a sign that He was so recognized.

Thus do we see that the fact that the Sabbath was a sign between God and the children of Israel, instead of being a reason why it should not be kept today, is one of the most important reasons why it should. Idolatry is spreading over all the earth today, and many of those who may be called idolaters accept the theory of evolution, which means the same as repudiating God as the Creator. So one can see that the observance of the Sabbath as a sign of belief in the literal creation, is more important today than ever before. The spread of idolatry accounts for God's bringing about such widespread proclamation of the Sabbath truth in this generation.

An opponent of the Sabbath once said, "I can believe that God is the creator without observing the Sabbath." So could Isaiah and all the other holy men of old. But why should they not express their belief by the observance of the Sabbath as a sign of their conviction, especially since God had commanded it?

A man may just as consistently argue that he can believe in the atonement and in the broken body and spilled blood of our Lord without observing the Lord's Supper. But it is a serious question whether such belief would be acceptable with God.

Sabbath observance has never ceased to be a sign of the recognition of God as the Creator. To illustrate: Today in all parts of the world Sabbathkeepers assemble for worship on the seventh day. Suppose someone going by such a house of worship on the seventh day should inquire: "Why do these people assemble on the seventh day?" The answer would be: "They do not believe in evolution. They believe that God created the world and everything in it in six days and rested on the seventh, and they observe every seventh day as a sign of that belief. If they did not believe this, they would not be assembled on this day." This would be a true statement of the case. We inquire: Was this truth—that God through His Son was the Creator—of intrinsic value to the Israelites in Old Testament times when all about them the world was filled with men worshiping idols? Was not the observance of the Sabbath a weekly reminder to the heathen as to who the true God was? Today, when the Genesis record of creation is almost universally thought of as a fable, when God is no longer recognized as the Creator, is not the observance of the Sabbath even more important? When it is kept as a sign of belief in creation, does it displease the Lord? Did this important duty of recognizing God as the Creator and the observance of the Sabbath as a sign of the recognition of that great truth terminate at the cross? Was it because there was nothing of essential value in the recognition of God as the Creator that the Lord is supposed to have discontinued the Sabbath at the cross? Where are the scriptures which so teach? They are not to be found.

We have already cited scriptures of the New Testament showing that when the apostles wished to introduce the true God at Lystra and Athens, as contrasted with the false gods which the pagans worshiped, they introduced Him to them as the Creator of the heavens and the earth. Apparently the recognition of the fact of God's creatorship did not cease at the cross, and neither did the memorial, which is a sign of this important truth. (Romans 3:31). As long as men should believe the Lord's creatorship was important, just so long should the Lord's true Sabbath day to be observed as a sign of that fundamental truth. Herein lies the intrinsic value of the Sabbath, together with the proof of its immutability.

Sabbath Also for Gentiles

Labored efforts are made by some to prove that Sabbath observance served only as a memorial of the deliverance from Egypt, and that since the Gentiles were not in the "deliverance" the Sabbath is not for them.

Then what about even the Jews who lived after that generation died? They had no part in that deliverance either.

We find the Lord saying (through Isaiah many centuries later) that the Sabbath was for Gentiles, too, although they had no part in the Egyptian bondage and deliverance. This we read in Isaiah 56:6, 7:

"Also the sons of the stranger, that join themselves to the Lord [not to the Jews] to serve him, and to love the name of the Lord, to be his servants, every one that keepeth the sabbath from polluting it, and taketh hold of my covenant; even them will I bring to my holy mountain, and make them joyful in my house of prayer."

These statements certainly overthrow the claim that the Sabbath was to be observed only by those who were delivered from Egypt. Turning to the New Testament, we read, "The Gentiles besought that these words might be preached to them the next sabbath." Their request was granted, "and the next sabbath day came almost the whole city together to hear the word of God." Acts 13:42, 44. This was more than a thousand years after the deliverance from Egypt.

We are now ready to examine the truth of Deuteronomy 5:15, which reads:

"And remember that thou wast a servant in the land of Egypt, and that the Lord thy God brought thee out thence through a mighty hand and by a stretched out arm: therefore the Lord thy God commanded thee to keep the sabbath day."

While God's people were in Egypt with taskmasters over them, they had no religious liberty; they were not allowed to keep the Sabbath. But now that they were out from under that bondage, they could keep the Sabbath and were "commanded" to do so. That this is what the Lord was directly talking about is brought out in verse fourteen:

"But the seventh day is the sabbath of the Lord thy God: in it thou shalt not do any work, thou, nor thy son, nor thy daughter, nor thy manservant, nor thy maidservant nor thine ox, nor thine ass, nor any of thy cattle, nor thy stranger that is within thy gates; that thy manservant and thy maidservant may rest as well as thou."

The last part of the verse, which has reference to the servants, is the key to the understanding of the next statement: "And remember that thou wast a servant in the land of Egypt." When it came to dealing with *their* servants, they were to *remember* when *they* were servants and deprived of religious liberty, and they were to be thoughtful to give *their* manservant and maidservant opportunity for worship. There was no further excuse from those who had been delivered for not keeping the Sabbath. They were no longer to work on that day. Neither were they to deprive their servants of the same privilege of Sabbath rest. Thus by putting verse fourteen with verse fifteen, we find that the real meaning is made plain.

We note a similar account in Leviticus 19:33, 34: "If a stranger sojourn with thee in your land, ye shall not vex him. . . . For ye were strangers in the land of Egypt." When the Sabbath came week by week, the children of Israel were not to treat strangers as they were treated in Egypt. The strangers were to be permitted to "keep the sabbath day" and not to be forced to work.

The Sabbath Before the Cross

In the attempt to prove that the Sabbath was for the Jews only, some strange arguments are used. Those who hold this view usually begin with the argument that there is no record of Sabbath observance from its institution in Genesis 2:1–3 until we reach the Jews in the book of Exodus. Of course if that argument were applied to the other nine commandments, it would mean that all those good men between Adam and Moses were liars, thieves, and profaners of the Lord's name because we cannot find where the Lord ever told them not to do these things.

It can be said, without any fear of contradiction, that the first day of the week was not even mentioned until twenty years after the day of Pentecost, and then it is not mentioned as a day to be observed, but as a working day. So in using the silence argument with reference to the seventh-day Sabbath, its opponents, at the same time, destroy all possibility of the first day being the Lord's day.

Then again, if first-day keepers could find that on the day of Pentecost the first day of the week was instituted, that God blessed and sanctified the first day of the week, the discovery would certainly be used by first-day advocates to prove it was the day observed from then onward, even though it were never mentioned again. But there is no such record of God's blessing and sanctifying the first day at that time, about twenty-seven years before it is mentioned in the book of Acts. It is a fact, however, that more than two thousand years before the Exodus movement the Sabbath was instituted. We read: "And God blessed the seventh day, and sanctified it: because that in it he had rested from all his works which God created and made." Genesis 2:3.

If the first-day advocates will not accept the silence argument with reference to the first day of the week, why bring it up with reference to the seventh? If they could read that the Lord instituted the first day of the week on the day of Pentecost, if they would use such a fact to prove it was to be ever afterward observed, why deny the same thing about the seventh?

Some Objections Examined

There are two objections offered with reference to the institution of the Sabbath in Genesis 2:3. One is this: "It was not called the Sabbath day." To this we would mention that Genesis 2:3 says, "God blessed the seventh day." And Exodus 20:11, speaking of this event, says, "The Lord blessed the sabbath day." So the Lord says it was the Sabbath day that He blessed. Thus He calls the seventh day of Genesis 2:3 "the sabbath day." The Hebrew word "sabbath" means "rest." It was the Lord's rest day from the time He rested on the seventh day of the creation week. So the Bible does call the seventh day the Sabbath day.

The second objection is that the Lord rested on the seventh day in Genesis 2:3, but He never blessed the day until over two thousand years later. Of course this argument is overthrown by Mark 2:27, where we read simply that "the sabbath was made." The making of the Sabbath is recorded in Genesis 2:2,3 and naturally required three things: (1) The Lord "rested" on the seventh day. (2) The Lord "blessed" the seventh day. (3) The Lord "sanctified" the seventh day. These considerations prove it was blessed at the time it was made for man, more than two thousand years before there was a Jew. Moreover, how would it sound to say that in Genesis 1:26 the Lord said, "Let us make man in our image," but it was more than two thousand years later that "God blessed them." How foolish!

If language means anything, especially in God's Word, it will convince anyone that there was in existence in some form a divine revelation which He called "my law," and this law enjoined the observance of Sabbath. In proof of this we quote the following: "Then said the Lord unto Moses, Behold, I will rain bread from heaven for you; and the people shall go out and gather a certain rate every day, that I may prove them, whether they will walk in my law, or no." Exodus 16:4.

Then concerning the gathering of the manna, the Lord said: "Six days ye shall gather it; but on the seventh day, which is the sabbath, in it there shall be none. And it came to pass, that there went out some of the people on the seventh day for to gather, and they found none. And the Lord said unto Moses, How long refuse ye to keep my commandments and my laws?" Exodus 16:26–28.

This chapter is dated "the fifteenth day of the second month after their departing out of the land of Egypt." Exodus 16:1. It was "in the third month" when they reached Sinai. (Exodus 19:1, 2). The Sabbath existed as a part of God's law before the law was proclaimed on Sinai. How long had it existed? In Exodus 20:11 we read that the seventh day of Genesis 2:3 is called "the sabbath day." Therefore, the Sabbath day has existed from creation. (Genesis 2:3). That is when it was made, and Jesus said, "The sabbath was made for man." Since man has existed since creation week, it is easy to see that the Sabbath was made for man more than two thousand years before there was a Jew.

But "their fathers"—Abraham, Isaac, and Jacob—were "commanded" to keep the Sabbath. This we find in Jeremiah 17:22: "But hallow ye the sabbath day, as I commanded your fathers." Then in Numbers 20:15 we read, "Our fathers went down into Egypt." That was centuries before the giving of the law on Sinai and proves the Sabbath was observed from the time it "was made for man."

The Sabbath Not Jewish

Thus there is no such institution known to the Bible as the Jewish Sabbath. The names given the Creator's rest day in the Bible are the following:

"The holy sabbath." Exodus 16:23.
"The sabbath of the Lord." Exodus 20:10.
"My holy day." Isaiah 58:13.
"The sabbath day according to the commandment." Luke 23:56.
"The seventh day." Hebrews 4:4.
"The Lord's day." Revelation 1:10.

All these terms separate the seventh day from all other days of the week. They show that the seventh day is a divine institution which belongs to the Lord. It is "the holy sabbath unto the Lord." Exodus 16:23. There is no intimation that it is in any sense a Jewish Sabbath. It was made for man long before the Jews lived. In point of need it applies to all mankind. In point of application it is in no sense distinctly national.

When a man is destitute of evidence against a proposition, he frequently resorts to derision, scorn, and ridicule to cheapen it in the estimation of those he is trying to influence. Now surely preachers ought to know that the Sabbath is not Jewish, and that Inspiration calls it "the sabbath of the Lord thy God." They know it is one of the Ten Commandments, the importance of which they teach until the Sabbath is brought up. Since this is the case, the only thing to do is to resort to derision and scorn and call it "the old Jewish Sabbath" to stigmatize its holy character.

This suggestive method has always been resorted to when there was nothing else to do. It was the method used by the Pharisees when they could not overthrow the teachings of Jesus. In their determination to get the best of the Master and glorify themselves in the eyes of the public, they gathered their ecclesiastical robes about them, assumed an expression of scorn on their faces, and said, "We be not born of fornication." John 8:41. How very mean that was! How sinister! How unfair! But it had its effect. It turned many away from Jesus and the truths which He taught.

With the same actions, feelings, and facial expressions of scorn and ridicule, and to carry a point which they are unable to prove by appeal to logic and evidence, men will today speak of "the old Jewish Sabbath." There is not one particle of difference between this method of turning people against the Lord's Sabbath and that used by the Pharisees to turn the people away from the Lord Himself.

Opponents of the Sabbath will read texts that mean the ceremonial law and scornfully apply them to the Sabbath and the Ten Commandments instead of reading such texts as these: "This is the love of God, that we keep his commandments." 1 John 5:3. "He that saith, I know him, and keepeth not his commandments, is a liar, and the truth is not in him." 1 John 2:4. "Blessed are they that do his commandments." Revelation 22:14. "And the dragon was wroth with the woman, and went to make war with the remnant of her seed, which keep the commandments of God." Revelation 12:17. "For whosoever shall keep the whole law, and yet offend in one point, he is guilty of all." James 2:10. "They returned, and prepared spices and ointments; and rested the sabbath day according to the commandment." Luke 23:56. "The Gentiles besought that these words might be preached to them the next sabbath." Acts 13:42. "And the next sabbath day came almost the whole city together to hear the word of God." Acts 13:44. "And God did rest the seventh day from all his works." Hebrews 4:4. "Circumcision is nothing, and uncircumcision is nothing, but the keeping of the commandments of God." 1 Corinthians 7:19. "Whosoever committeth sin transgresseth also the law: for sin is the transgression of the law." 1 John 3:4. "Nay, I had not known sin, but by the law." Romans 7:7. These are inspired words of the living God supporting the sanctity of the Sabbath, which mistaken people scornfully oppose by calling it "the old Jewish Sabbath."

One great truth which the Word of God repeatedly states is that "there is no respect of persons with God." It was the purpose of God that the nations about the Israelites should "hear all these statutes." (Deuteronomy 4:6). And as the Gentiles were converted to the true God and became members of the church in the days of Moses and the prophets, they were to enjoy the spiritual blessings of the Sabbath. This conversion from heathenism to the true God and His truth meant that the converts were to "join themselves to the Lord." Then the Sabbath blessing was for them as well as for the Jews. In proof of this we quote Isaiah 56:6, 7: "Also the sons of the stranger, that join themselves to the Lord, to serve him, and to love the name of the Lord, to be his servants, every one that keepeth the sabbath from polluting it, and taketh hold of my covenant; even them will I bring to my holy mountain, and make them joyful in my house of prayer."

In the presence of such evidence, how can a man claim to be informed and at the same time contend that the Sabbath was only for Israel? How can it be dogmatically contended that "in the Old Testament ages no provisions were made, so far as Scripture records, for Gentile needs"?

"True enough," objectors will state, "but they had to join themselves to the Israelites, to be under obligation to observe the Sabbath." We reply, Did that keep them from being Gentiles? Did that change them from fleshly Gentiles to fleshly Jews? Certainly not.

To claim that the Gentiles must join themselves to the Israelites before the Sabbath can be for them is just like saying, "A man must become a Christian before the observance of the Lord's Supper can be for him"—which is true, since a man cannot become a Christian without, at the same time, accepting the atonement, for which the Lord's Supper stands.

Before they were converted to the true God, the strangers worshiped false gods. As long as they worshiped those gods, it would be just as inconsistent for them to observe the Sabbath as it would be for an unbeliever in the atonement to observe the Lord's Supper. But when those idolaters were converted to the truth, the Bible says they were to "join themselves to the Lord," "to love the name of the Lord," "to be his servants," "to serve him." (Isaiah 56:6).

God Is No Respecter of Persons

When this union with the true God took place, certainly the Sabbath was for those Gentiles. As soon as they had forsaken their idols and were converted to the true God, who "hath made the earth by his power," they were to keep the Sabbath as an acknowledgment of their allegiance to the true God, which "made heaven and earth, the sea, and all that in them is." Already to Moses the Lord had repeatedly said, "one law and one manner shall be for you, and for the stranger that sojourneth with you." Numbers 15:16. See also Exodus 12:49; Numbers 9:14. In the presence of such evidence, how can one claim that the Sabbath was for Israel and not for the Gentiles?

When Solomon's temple was finished, and the time came for the dedicatory prayer, God inspired Solomon to include the converted Gentiles among those who would come up to the temple to worship. Solomon proclaimed: "Moreover concerning the stranger, which is not of thy people, but is come from a far country for thy great name's sake, and thy mighty hand, and thy stretched out arm; if they come and pray in this house; then hear thou from the heavens, even from thy dwelling place, and do according to all that the stranger calleth to thee for; that all people of the earth may know thy name, and fear thee, as doth thy people Israel." 2 Chronicles 6:32, 33.

Does this make provision for "Gentile needs"?

The no-law teachers hold that Romans 2:11–15 proves that the Sabbath was for none but the Jews. We quote:

"For there is no respect of persons with God. For as many as have sinned without law shall also perish without law; and as many as have sinned in the law shall be judged by the law; (For not the hearers of the law are just before God, but the doers of the law shall be justified. For when the Gentiles, which have not the law, do by nature the things contained in the law, these, having not the law, are a law unto themselves:

which shew the work of the law written in their hearts, their conscience also bearing witness, and their thoughts the mean while accusing or else excusing one another)."

Paul is here contrasting those who had a knowledge of the written law with the heathen who did not. Those who had a knowledge of the written law would be judged by that standard. Those who did not would be judged according to how they had related themselves to the principles of the same law. When Paul uses the expression "the Gentiles, which have not the law," he has reference to those who had no knowledge of God's written Word and law. Why say it means that the law was not for them, and that when God said not to steal, lie, commit adultery, or worship idols, He meant that the Gentiles were not to regulate their conduct thereby? The no-lawists' argument is that no matter how well acquainted the Gentiles had become with the Word of God and His law, they were in the sight of God free to steal, lie, blaspheme the name of the Lord, and violate the rest of the commandments without coming under condemnation, since the law was only for the Jews. And all just to avoid the commandment which says, "The seventh day is the sabbath of the Lord thy God."!

That the law was for "all the world" is plainly stated by the Apostle Paul in Romans 3:19: "Now we know that what things soever the law saith, it saith to them who are under the law: that every mouth may be stopped, and all the world may become guilty before God." The expressions "all the world" and "every mouth" certainly include all the people in the world, whether they be Jews or not. Therefore, whatever the law said to the Jews, it said also to all the world. Then it says to all the world and not to the Jews only, "The seventh day is the sabbath."

Consider this carefully: When Jesus came, was it only the Jews who were guilty before God and needed redemption from the sentence of death because of transgression? Were not the Gentiles under the same condemnation? Did not Paul say, "They are all under sin"; and, "All have sinned"? All were "under the law" in the sense that they were "guilty before God." (Romans 3:9, 19). So if all the world includes the Gentiles, they were just as amenable to the law (as far as they understood it) as were the Jews. Then, since this law made provision for the observance of the Sabbath, does this not prove that it was for them, too?

But to settle beyond all dispute the fact that the law was for the Gentiles, as well as for the Jews, let us read Leviticus 24:16: "He that blasphemeth the name of the Lord, he shall surely be put to death, and all the congregation shall certainly stone him: as well the stranger [Gentile], as he that is born in the land, when he blasphemeth the name of the Lord, shall be put to death." Let us understand this: The third commandment said, "Thou shalt not take the name of the Lord thy God in vain." In order to avoid the fact that the Sabbath was for the Gentiles as well as for the Jews, it is contended that the Ten Commandment law was for the Jews only, and not in any sense was its violation by the Gentiles subject to divine punishment. In Leviticus 24:16, however, we have a strong contradiction of this claim. When the Gentiles presumptuously blasphemed the name of the Lord, the same penalty was meted out to them as to the Jews. Now for a question: If the Gentiles really were not amenable to this law, if "what things soever the law saith" it said to the Jews only, why was the transgression of it by the Gentiles punished just the same as transgression by the Jews? Will those who claim that this law was for the Jews only explain this? Then, if the Gentiles were held accountable for violating the third commandment, were they not held equally accountable for the violation of the fourth?

Sunday School Lessons Use All but "Seventh"

It is interesting to notice how those who *theoretically* abolish the fourth commandment will turn right around, on certain occasions, and hold to the wording of all of it, except one word. That one word is "seventh." About once a year the International Sunday School lesson is on "Sabbath Observance," or "Sunday Observance," and in it this practice is followed.

In looking over the lessons in fundamentalist periodicals, one finds that every text quoted as to how Sunday should be observed applies not to the first, but to the seventh day of the week. Such statements as "call the sabbath a delight," "remember the sabbath day, to keep it holy," "lawful to do well on the sabbath days," etc., are cited in the lesson comments and then applied to a day that God has never mentioned in reference to such instructions. How very illogical it is to condemn the fourth commandment and then go to the same commandment and pick out all the words in it, except the word "seventh," and apply them to the first day of the week! In other words the whole of that commandment is accepted and taught except the one word "seventh," although the commandment exclusively refers to the day of that number. It would be just as logical for a pagan to pick out every word in the Bible with reference to the worship of the true God and then apply the instructions to the manner in which his pagan god should be worshiped. The wording of the Sabbath commandment has definitely no reference to Sunday.

Man cannot make a day holy and sacred simply by the application of holy titles. Can anyone find in all the Bible where it says the instructions given with reference to the seventh day should be applied to the first? Then when man does that, is he not transferring titles? Can man take the coverings of the Sabbath marked "sanctified," "holy," "blessed," and "hallowed," and put them on the first day of the week? Can man find where God has ever done this? If not, where is the verse which gives him the authority to take these instructions as to the observance of the seventh day and place them on the first day? Let us remember what Jesus said, "The true worshippers shall worship the Father in spirit and in truth." John 4:23. To take the words which God has used with reference to the observance of the seventh day and misapply them to the first is not according to truth.

True Sabbathkeeping Not Physical

To illustrate the truth that proper Sabbath observance must include a state of mind which recognizes the sacredness of the day, I recall a certain lady who was well educated, but was blind and a helpless invalid. She could not even feed herself or use any of her limbs. A Bible teacher gave her some studies, among them one on the Sabbath and its observance. The lady accepted what she was taught. When it was reported in the neighborhood that she was going to keep the seventh day of the week, the talk was, "She does not work any day. She keeps every day." People could not understand how she could keep the Sabbath in any distinct way.

But she certainly did. She would inquire as to the time the sun was setting, and then she would think of the hours as sacred and so consider them until the setting of the sun the next evening. Such feeling of respect has a scriptural rather than a hereditary basis. The Word of God says, "The Lord blessed the sabbath day, and hallowed it." But there is not a word in the Bible which says the Lord made holy or hallowed the first day of the week. That being the case, it is impossible to observe the first day as a holy day.

Sabbath and Marriage

During Israel's wandering in the wilderness there were certain regulations concerning marriage that Jesus did not sanction when He came, but that does not mean that He abolished the institution itself. So there were certain regulations with reference to the observance of the Sabbath which Jesus did not sanction, but He did not abolish the institution itself. When Jesus came, He found both institutions existing, and He honored both and abolished neither.

The Creator made human beings in the beginning with a capacity for social fellowship and for spiritual fellowship. The capacity for human fellowship finds its most complete satisfaction and happiness in the marriage relationship and the home. The capacity for divine fellowship finds its most complete satisfaction in the Sabbath and the church. Both these institutions grew out of divinely implanted longings of the human heart. This being the case, God make provision for the perpetuation of the home and the Sabbath, because there will never come a time when these desires of the human heart will be destroyed. In His law of love God made provision for the sanctity of marriage when He said, "Thou shalt not commit adultery." He made provision for the perpetuity and sanctity of the Sabbath in the same law when He said, "Remember the sabbath day, to keep it holy."

The devil has always sought to pervert both of these divine institutions: to substitute in the place of one, pagan licentiousness; and in the place of the other, the pagan "day of the sun." The Sabbath is no more exclusively Jewish than is marriage. Both grew out of inherent needs or God-given capacities for human and divine fellowship. That makes them just as universal as is mankind.

In the earth made new there will be no marriage or giving in marriage; no children will be born. Those who will live there are being "born again" now, but social fellowship one with another will never cease. The Sabbath will continue through all future ages for a reminder of the creative and redemptive power of God and for spiritual fellowship. In Revelation 22:1, 2 we read: "And he shewed me a pure river of water of life, clear as crystal, proceeding out of the throne of God and of the Lamb. In the midst of the street of it, and on either side of the river, was there the tree of life, which bare twelve manner of fruits, and yielded her fruit every month." And Isaiah 66:23 says, "It shall come to pass, that from one new moon to another, and from one sabbath to another, shall all flesh come to worship before me, saith the Lord."

Accountable for Light

Of course there will be many in heaven who in this life never kept the true Sabbath. They fell asleep without knowing the truth which has been presented from the Scripture in these pages. To the enlightened but disobedient, the Lord says, "If ye were blind, ye should have no sin: but now ye say, We see; therefore your sin remaineth." John 9:41. Those who were blind will be judged according to their light, and the willfully disobedient, according to their folly.

Let us keep in mind that "sin is the transgression of the law." 1 John 3:4. But the gracious promise is, "If we confess our sins, he is faithful and just to forgive us our sins, and to cleanse us from all unrighteousness." 1 John 1:9.

Can you honestly before God say that you are blind to the light that the seventh day is the Sabbath of the Lord? Will you not thank God for revealing to you the truth as to the true Sabbath, and from now on, through the indwelling Christ, "remember the sabbath day, to keep it holy"?

Surely when the heavenly Father through His Son made the Sabbath for man even before sin entered this world, He did so in order to provide a day of rest and worship for mankind forever. And in the world to come some of the sweetest memories of this life will have to do with the spiritual refreshings which came to us in Sabbath assemblies, when everything was conducive to contemplation of the past, present, and future love of God, who, through His Son, provided the future life that we will then be enjoying, and to which there shall be no end.

Chapter 6

The Sabbath and the First Day of the Week

There is abundant evidence that the apostles kept the seventh day of the week, not the first. Jesus commanded its observance, and at one time said to the disciples, "But pray ye that your flight be not in the winter, neither on the sabbath day." Matthew 24:20. He was talking to them about the destruction of Jerusalem, which would take place thirty-nine years after Jesus had gone back to heaven in A.D. 70

The instruction as to the Sabbath day given in Matthew 24:20 came about this way: Jesus and His disciples were in Jerusalem. Pointing to the great temple there, the Saviour said to the disciples, "There shall not be left here one stone upon another, that shall not be thrown down." Wishing to know more about this, "the disciples came unto him privately, saying, Tell us, when shall these things be? and what shall be the sign of thy coming, and of the end of the world" Matthew 24:2, 3.

In this chapter Jesus answers both questions. A part of the time He was telling them about the signs of the destruction of Jerusalem, and a part of the time He was telling them about the signs of His coming. Speaking of the destruction of Jerusalem by the Romans in A.D. 70, Jesus said: "Then let them which be in Judaea flee into the mountains: let him which is on the housetop not come down to take any thing out of his house: neither let him which is in the field return back to take his clothes. And woe to them that are with child, and to them that give suck in those days! But pray ye that your flight be not in the winter, neither on the sabbath day." Matthew 24:16–20.

Jesus was talking here of the Sabbath day and its observance many years after the cross. This proves it did not cease to exist at the cross, any more than the winter ceased to exist then.

Because of the *hardships*, Christians were to pray that this "flight be not in the winter." Because of the *sacredness*, they were to pray that their flight be "not on the sabbath day." To any honest heart this proves that in the recognition of Jesus, there would still be a day after the cross known as the Sabbath day.

All sorts of crude and absurd arguments have been given by opponents of the Sabbath as to why Jesus here said what He did about the Sabbath day. One argument is that the gates were shut, and they could not get out. But the instruction was to all Judea. Was there a wall around Judea?

Something else: Jesus did not tell them to pray that they would not have to flee on the Day of Atonement, the day of Pentecost, or any of the other holy days of the Levitical law. These were passed over. They were done away at the cross. He did not tell them to pray about the first day of the week either. Sunday came week by week along with the Sabbath day, but it, too, was passed by in silence. Not so with the Sabbath. Suppose Jesus had said, "Pray that your flight be not on the first day of the week." How tenaciously His words would be clung to as an evidence that Sunday is the day for Christians to observe!

The Sabbath in the Book of Acts

Next we go to the book of Acts, and there we read more about the apostles and the Sabbath day. Of course the opponents of the Sabbath claim that the only reason the apostles attended worship on this day was to gain access to the Jews, and not because they had any regard for the sacredness of the day. But they offer no text to prove their contention. On the other hand we find the record that the apostles preached to the Gentiles on this day, too. Will it be claimed that these Gentiles were Sabbath observers and Paul met with them just to get the opportunity to preach to them? Such a claim is not made, for it would be too absurd. The Gentiles were not observers of the seventh day until after they became Christians.

In Acts 13:42 we find the following interesting statement: "And when the Jews were gone out of the synagogue, the Gentiles besought that these words might be preached to them the next sabbath." This text shows again that the Sabbath as a day of worship had not ceased at the cross, but was still reverenced week by week; and this was many years after the cross.

We read further: "Now when the congregation was broken up, many of the Jews and religious proselytes followed Paul and Barnabas: who,

speaking to them persuaded them to continue in the grace of God. And the next sabbath day came almost the whole city together to hear the word of God." Verses 43, 44. This meeting was requested by the Gentiles, and the text says "almost the whole city [came] together." In the face of this, what becomes of the human speculation that the only reason Paul held Sabbath meetings was to get to preach to the Jews? If, at that time, the first day of the week was the day to come together to hear the Word of God, why did not Paul say to the Gentiles, "No, not the next Sabbath. That has been abolished. You Gentiles come on the first day of the week." If such had been the case, he surely would have said so.

We go next to Acts 16:13, where we find Paul and Luke at Philippi. Luke said, "And on the sabbath we went out of the city by a river side, where prayer was wont to be made; and we sat down, and spake unto the women which resorted thither." Let it be remembered that Luke was not a Jew. Using the vocabulary of Gentile Christians at that time, he spoke of the seventh day and called it by its God-given name, "the sabbath." To this Christian man the Sabbath was still an existing institution.

At Corinth, where a church was raised up, Paul was employed at his craft. He found some Jewish friends, "and because he was of the same craft, he abode with them, and wrought: for by their occupation they were tentmakers. Now for a question: Did he rest on the first day or the seventh day—which? The answer is plain: "And he reasoned in the synagogue every sabbath, and persuaded the Jews and the Greeks." Acts 18:3, 4. Here we see that when the Sabbath came, Paul did not work.

Please note again Luke does not say "the Sabbath of the Jews." Luke, being a Gentile, made a custom of pointing out things which were exclusively Jewish. Note the following: "nation of the Jews" (Acts 10:22); "land of the Jews" (Acts 10:39); "people of the Jews" (Acts 12:11); and "synagogue of the Jews" (Acts 14:1). But where does he say "Sabbath of the Jews"? The fact that he not once says "Sabbath of the Jews," though he refers to the Sabbath over and over, seems to prove that he did not so consider it, and that those who claim it is exclusively Jewish are wrong.

Two Uses of the Word "Day"

Before taking up the "first day" question, I believe it is very important that we find out when the Bible says a day begins and ends. The word "day" in the creation account (as applied to the twenty-four-hour day) is used in two ways. First, the hours of dark and the hours of light are called a day: "The evening [the beginning of the dark part] and the morning [the beginning of the light part] were the sixth day." Genesis 1:31. That is a twenty-four hour day. Secondly, the light part is called day: "And God called the light Day." Genesis 1:5.

The Biblical Day

All through the Old and New Testaments a day, whether it be the first or seventh or any other, begins at evening and ends at evening; and the evening begins at the setting of the sun. In speaking of the Day of Atonement in Leviticus 23:27, 28, the Lord stated: "Also on the tenth day of the seventh month there shall be a day of atonement. . . . And ye shall do no work in that same day." This day had a starting and an ending time; for we read, "It shall be unto you a [yearly] sabbath of rest, . . . in the ninth day of the month at even [evening], from even unto even, shall ye celebrate your sabbath." Verse 32. The Israelites were to celebrate the tenth day of the month as a yearly sabbath. This tenth day began the ninth day at evening. Right up unto the evening, the day before was called the ninth day. But as soon as evening came and the light part of the ninth day was gone, the tenth day commenced. Get this, please: If the ninth day of the tenth month, at evening, introduces the tenth day, then the first day of the week at evening would introduce the second day of the week. It could not be otherwise because the first day would close at evening, and the second day would then begin.

I am bringing out this point right here so that all may be ready to understand John 20:19, which reads: "Then the same day at evening, being the first day of the week, when the doors were shut where the disciples were assembled for fear of the Jews, came Jesus and stood in the midst, and saith unto them, Peace be unto you." Some persons argue that it was still the first day of the week that night when Jesus came in. They contend this because John says, "At evening, being the first day of the week." No one will deny that the text reads this way. But it was the first day of the week at evening, and that would introduce the second day of the week. The first day of the week terminates at evening, and at the same time it brings in the second day of the week. If "the ninth day of the month at even" is the tenth day of the month, then "the first day of the week" at "evening" is the second day of the week—and all the wrangling of men who hold otherwise does not disprove it. Anyway, the disciples were meeting "for fear of the Jews," John says, and not to celebrate the resurrection. A novice in the Scriptures knows full well that at the time Jesus came in, the disciples did not believe He had been raised from the dead. Luke says that when Jesus came in, "they were terrified and affrighted, and supposed that they had seen a spirit." (Luke 24:36–41).

I will next prove that "evening" means "at the going down of the sun." We read: "But at the place which the Lord thy God shall choose to place his name in, there thou shalt sacrifice the passover at even [evening], at the going down of the sun." Deuteronomy 16:6. This text makes it plain that a Bible day is from sunset to sunset. Another scripture pointing out the same truth reads: "And afterward Joshua smote them, and slew them, and hanged them on five trees: and they were hanging upon the trees until the evening. And it came to pass at the time of the going down of the sun, that Joshua commanded, and they took them down." Joshua 10:26, 27.

Coming now to the New Testament, we find the same reckoning. The beginning and ending of a day is based on planetary arrangement as found in the first chapter of Genesis—and the death of Jesus never changed the movements of the planets which bring night and day. So we read in Mark 1:32: "And at even, when the sun did set." And Paul, in Ephesians 4:26, said, "Let not the sun go down upon your wrath"—in other words, don't take the sins of one day over into another. He did not say, "And let not midnight go down on your wrath." To Paul the next day came on when the sun went down.

There are those who claim it is a sin to take the Lord's Supper and to take up a collection on any other day than the first day of the week; yet these people will do these things after the sun goes down on Sunday night, which makes it the second day of the week.

The First Day in the Gospels

We will next notice what Matthew, Mark, Luke, and John have to say about the first day of the week. They were to go and teach men, Jesus said, to observe "all things whatsoever I have commanded you." We find where Jesus taught about baptism, the Lord's Supper, the Sabbath, and many other things. But nowhere did Jesus ever "command" the disciples to observe the resurrection day and to take the Lord's Supper on that day. In fact we are safe in saying that not once during all His ministry did Jesus ever mention the first day of the week. And His followers did not teach others to observe it.

Luke

Luke, a Gentile Christian, was especially qualified to tell us all about what Jesus practiced and taught. Luke says he had "perfect understanding of all things from the very first." (Luke 1:3) Moreover he said that in his gospel he gives us a "treatise" of "all that Jesus began both to do and to teach" (Acts 1:1). So that the fact that we find nothing in the book of Luke about Jesus ever once mentioning the first day of the week is positive proof that He never gave any command on that point, and that explains why we find nothing in the apostolic preaching on Sunday observance.

Luke 23:56 tells how the Christians "rested the sabbath day according to the commandment." Following this, Luke states, "Upon the first day of the week, very early in the morning they came to the sepulchre." They wanted to finish the work which was left unfinished Friday evening, and they found that Jesus was risen. Luke had a good chance here to say something about the first day of the week taking the place of "the sabbath day according to the commandment." It is important to remember that Luke said the things which have just been quoted in A.D. 63, which was about thirty years after Jesus returned to heaven. So thirty years after the cross this Gentile Christian was still calling the seventh day "the sabbath" and the resurrection day "the first day of the week." So at that time he was not calling the first day of the week the Lord's day.

Matthew

Having found that Luke gives no hint of first-day sacredness, we will next see what Matthew, Mark, and John have to say. Matthew 28:1 reads, "In the end of the sabbath, as it began to dawn toward the first day of the week, came Mary Magdalene and the other Mary to see the sepulchre." The Emphatic Diaglott Greek New Testament reads: "Now after the Sabbath, as it was *dawning* to the first day of the week." Matthew wrote this a good many years after it happened. He still called the seventh day "the sabbath" and the next day "the first day of the week."

Mark

Coming to Mark 16:1, 2, 9, we find this apostle mentioning Sunday twice. He says, "And when the sabbath was past . . . very early in the morning the first day of the week, they came unto the sepulchre"; and verse nine says, "Jesus was risen early the first day of the week." When

Mark wrote this, in A.D. 60, some twenty-seven years after the cross, he was still calling Sunday the first day of the week and was not using some sacred title for the day. He also says that when this day comes, the Sabbath is past.

John

John speaks of the first day of the week twice. In John 20:1 he writes, "The first day of the week cometh Mary Magdalene early, when it was yet dark, unto the sepulchre, and seeth the stone taken away from the sepulchre." John wrote this in A.D. 100, and at that time he called Sunday the first day of the week. He wrote the book of Revelation four years before, and in Revelation 1:10 he says he was "in the Spirit on the Lord's day." He had reference to the day the Lord has always claimed as His from the creation of the world, at which time the Lord "blessed the sabbath day, and hallowed it." If John held that the first day of the week had become the Lord's day, he certainly would have called it that four years later when telling about the resurrection.

John's second mention of the first day of the week is found in John 20:19: "The same day at evening, being the first day of the week, when the doors were shut where the disciples were assembled for fear of the Jews, came Jesus and stood in the midst, and saith unto them, Peace be unto you." Here again John had an opportunity to call Sunday the Lord's day, but the fact that he did not shows he never thought of it as such.

"After Eight Days"

There is one more text which is claimed to have reference to the first day of the week. It is John 20:26–28: "And after eight days again his disciples were within, and Thomas was with them: then came Jesus, the doors being shut, and stood in the midst, and said, Peace be unto you. Then saith he to Thomas, Reach hither thy finger, and behold my hands; and reach hither thy hand, and thrust it into my side: and be not faithless, but believing. And Thomas answered and said unto him, My Lord and my God."

There is no way to prove this was the first day of the week. Even if it were, Jesus came there, not to celebrate the day, but to convince Thomas that He was alive. Jesus told the disciples not to depart from Jerusalem but to tarry there for the coming of the Holy Spirit. They "abode" there in "an upper room." And during the forty days that Jesus stayed on the earth before returning to heaven, He was "seen of them forty days" (Act 1:3). So if appearing to them in that upper room made those days holy days, then that would make all forty of those days holy. If the evidence some men are trying to discover to prove Sunday to be the Lord's day were not so scarce, they certainly would not use such "proofs."

The words "after eight days" are very indefinite. Speaking of the transfiguration, Matthew says, "After six days Jesus taketh Peter, James, and John his brother, and bringeth them up into an high mountain apart." Matthew 17:1. What is meant "after six days"? Luke gives us an inspired answer: "And it came to pass about an eight days after these saying, he took Peter and John and James, and went up into a mountain to pray. Luke 9:28. So the Bible statement "after six days" means "about eight days after." Thus when John says "after eight days," it could have been ten days after. No one knows which day it was. The Bible does not tell us.

Let us consider now a statement that is often made by Sunday-keepers: "After His resurrection Jesus met with His disciples again and again to celebrate the resurrection with them." All the facts are against such a statement. He never met with them for such a purpose on any occasion that we have record of. One text says He met with them on the first day of the week after evening had come on, and that would make it the second day of the week. And at this time they were afraid and did not believe He was alive.

The First Day in Apostolic Literature

Having proved to any honest heart just when the first day of the week begins and ends, I am now ready to examine some of the places where this day is mentioned in the apostolic writings, and prove that it was a working day—just as it started out to be in the first chapter of Genesis. Many preachers will read the first statement in Acts 20:7, which says, "And upon the first day of the week, when the disciples came together to break bread," and will stop. They handle these words in a way as to lead their hearers to believe that this meeting occurred on a Sunday morning about eleven o'clock, and that it was repeated every week at the same time. I have never yet heard one of them finish even the first sentence, which ends, "And continued his speech until midnight." They also omit the rest of the story, which says: "And there were many lights in the upper chamber, where they were gathered together." So it was a night meeting held on the dark part of the first day of the week. The account continues: "And there sat in a window a certain young man named Eutychus, being fallen into a deep sleep: and as Paul was long preaching, he sank down with sleep, and fell down from the third loft, and was taken up dead. And Paul went down, and fell on him, and embracing him said, Trouble not yourselves; for his life is in him." Here it was after midnight, and the breaking of the bread had not yet taken place. Let us read on: "When he therefore was come up again, and had broken bread, and eaten, and talked a long while, even till break of day, so he departed."

The First Day a Work Day

We shall now prove that Luke and the others who were travelling with Paul were working hard taking the ship around the peninsula to Assos while Paul was holding this all-night farewell meeting with the believers at Troas; that they would not leave with the ship until the Sabbath closed at sunset. Luke, after writing an account of this farewell service and the Lord's Supper between midnight and break of day, says, "And we [Luke and the others except Paul] went before to ship, and sailed unto Assos, there intending to take in Paul: for so had he appointed, minding himself to go afoot. And when he met with us at Assos, we took him in, and came to Mitylene." Acts 20:13, 14. Notice Luke states, "We went before to ship, and sailed unto Assos." We ask, Before what? Well, what was he talking about? He was talking about that all-night meeting and what had happened. So the fact that they went on in the ship before that meeting shows they were not present, and that they were hard at work taking the ship around. Notice, too, that was as Paul had "appointed," which means he gave them the orders to work on Sunday.

A well-known no-lawist agrees with Sabbathkeepers that this meeting at Troas took place on Saturday night. He says: "The brethren met in the early part of the night, yet it was 'the first day of the week.' We have no evidence that either Jews or Gentiles had yet adopted the custom of counting the hours from midnight. Consequently we must suppose that the night in question . . . was Saturday night." He goes on to say, "At daybreak the meeting terminated in one of those tender farewells so often spoken of among believers. It was a night never to be forgotten." So the whole story can be summed up in one sentence: They had a special all-night farewell meeting on the night part of the first day of the week and broke bread together between midnight and dawn. The facts are all against this being a regular weekly custom.

Observance of the Lord's Supper

Just here is a good place to see what Paul says about the time of the observance of the Lord's Supper. In 1 Corinthians 11:2 Paul says, "Now I praise you, brethren, that ye remember me in all things, and keep the ordinances, as I delivered them to you." Note the words "as I delivered them to you." Then Paul says, "I have received of the Lord that which also I delivered unto you." Verse 23. Now if we can find out what he delivered, we can at the same time find out what he received, and see whether he received from the Lord anything about the first day of the week being the time. So we read on, "For as often as ye eat this bread, and drink this cup, ye do shew the Lord's death till he come." Verse 26. So that leaves it up to the option of the church as to when the Lord's Supper shall be celebrated. For the text says, "As often as ye eat this bread, and drink this cup." Get this: Paul says he delivered what he received. The fact that he never delivered anything about the first day of the week being the time is positive proof that he never received any such instruction from the Lord. That is evident to any honest reader.

Paul could not possibly have stated that the first day of the week is the only proper time for the observance of the Lord's Supper, for if he had, he would have condemned the Lord and His disciples. For he says:

"The Lord Jesus the same night [Thursday night] in which he was betrayed took bread: and when he had given thanks, he brake it, and said, Take, eat: this is my body, which is broken for you: this do in remembrance of me. After the same manner also he took the cup, when he had supped, saying, This cup is the new testament in my blood: this do ye, as oft as ye drink it, in remembrance of me." 1 Corinthians 11:23–25.

So Paul quotes Jesus as saying, "As oft as ye drink it"—which certainly leaves out any weekly, first-day-of-the-week arrangement. If Sunday is the only time, then Jesus and His disciples made a mistake. Instead of taking it on Thursday night, as they did, they should have waited until the first day of the week. I am not prepared to involve the Redeemer in a mistake.

Pentecost

Another argument which I have heard used with a great deal of triumph is the claim that, since Pentecost fell on the first day of the week and the Holy Spirit was poured out on that day, therefore the first day is the Christian Sabbath. But the question of which day of the week was Pentecost has no relevance whatever to the question of which day is the Sabbath.

The Sabbath was made by the act of God in resting from creation on the seventh day, and blessing and sanctifying that day. That act was announced to the human race by the voice of God Himself from Sinai. That divine fiat has never with equal formality been abrogated. There has been no comparable enactment making the day on which the Holy Spirit was given the Christian Sabbath. Until such a legislative act by Deity sanctifying the first day is produced, we maintain that no event of whatever magnitude occurring on the first day can constitute it the Sabbath in place of the day decreed by the Creator, Lawgiver, and Judge.

This same logic applies to the argument that the occurrence of the resurrection on the first day of the week constitutes that day the Christian Sabbath. The importance of the event taking place on the day is not what makes it the Sabbath. It is the legislative act of God. That law of God specifies the seventh day, not the first, no matter what has happened since on the first day of the week.

Collections on the First Day

It is indeed tragic that people can believe and practice something which would immediately be given up if they would only do a little investigating. There are multitudes who believe that the New Testament actually teaches that people should come together on the first day of the week and take up a collection. Some go so far as to contend that a collection should not be taken up at any other time. From the pulpit ministers will say, "Paul says we should lay by in store on the first day of the week." It never occurs to them that Paul did not word it that way. He said, "Let every one of you [individually] lay by him in store." But the preacher never says, "Lay by him." He leaves the "him" out. The words "lay by him" mean that the collecting was done at home and not at a religious gathering. If a person puts his offering in a collection plate, he would be doing the very opposite.

Incidentally, Paul was not speaking of a congregational church collection at all. He was speaking of a famine relief fund which was to be sent to "the poor saints . . . at Jerusalem." In the early Pentecostal days many of the believers "sold their possessions and goods, and parted them to all men, as every man had need." Acts 2:45. Later a famine came, and the

Lord was looking out for these generous souls. We read of this in Acts 11:27–30.

"And in these days came prophets from Jerusalem unto Antioch. And there stood up one of them named Agabus, and signified by the Spirit that there should be great dearth throughout all the world: which came to pass in the days of Claudius Caesar. Then the disciples, every man according to his ability, determined to send relief unto the brethren which dwelt in Judaea: which also they did, and sent it to the elders by the hands of Barnabas and Saul."

Please notice the words "dearth" and "relief." Turning to Romans 15:26, we find more about this relief fund: "For it hath pleased them of Macedonia and Achaia to make a certain contribution for the poor saints which are at Jerusalem." This boils it down to a certain relief contribution. The word "certain" here makes it sure that this was not a regular practice every Sunday. In Acts 27:16 we read of a "certain island." Thus it is distinguished from other islands. So a certain contribution would distinguish it from other contributions. All of which proves it was not a regular weekly congregational collection.

We are now ready to read 1 Corinthians 16:1–3 with a true understanding of what Paul was thinking when he wrote: "Now concerning the collection for the saints." You ask, Which saints? We already have found the answer—the "poor saints . . . at Jerusalem. Let us read on: "As I have given order to the churches of Galatia." Those orders were given when it was learned the dearth was coming—which proves it was not something already being practiced every Sunday, else it would not have been necessary for him to issue such orders. "Upon the first day of the week let every one of you lay by him in store." A recent version of the New Testament reads: "Let each of you put aside at home." The words "lay by him" certainly could not have reference to a church collection plate. The words "in store" could only mean that the disciple was adding to this fund week by week until Paul arrived. We read on: "As God hath prospered him." This is why this laying "by him in store" was to be done on the first day of the week, a working day, instead of it being done on the Sabbath day.

Corinth was a seaport town, and if some of the brethren were merchants, it would not be in harmony with Sabbath observance to be figuring out how much the goods had cost, the profits made on the sales, the expenses for rents, clerk hire, etc. All this would be necessary in order to find out how "God hath prospered him." Since the business part of the week closed at sunset on the sixth day of the week, he was then to close shop and forget his material matters over the Sabbath. But when the first day of the week came, it was time to begin work again, and then he carried out the orders of Paul by going over all the business of the past week to see how God had prospered him. Then each week he laid by him in store more and more until Paul arrived. Paul said this was to be done so they could individually have something stored up, "that there be no gatherings" when he came. They would, each one, have something saved up and could bring it and place it in his hands, and he would not have to go around from house to house to see what he could gather up. "And when I come, whomsoever ye shall approve by your letters, them will I send to bring your liberality unto Jerusalem. And if it be meet that I go also, they shall go with me." This is what happened, as we read in Acts 11:30: "Which also they did, and sent it to the elders by the hands of Barnabas and Saul."

Now in the face of all these simple facts about this certain contribution for this relief fund, how very deceptive it is to take advantage of the ignorance of a Sunday morning congregation to make the believe this was a regular congregational collection for the local preacher and church, and that it gives proof of first-day sacredness. The fact is that there was no such thing going on at Corinth, and the record shows that it was a day of figuring up accounts relating to secular business.

"The Day Which the Lord Hath Made"

Before closing this chapter on the first day of the week, I have been trying to think of some other "arguments" I have heard. I happen to recall two which have not been mentioned. They are so farfetched that it seems impossible that any should have ever thought of them. There is a verse in Psalm 118:24 which says, "This is the day which the Lord hath made; we will rejoice and be glad in it."

This text is read, and then a great deal is said about the first day of the week, the day on which Jesus arose, being a day of gladness and rejoicing to the women and the disciples. Thus there is much ado about nothing, for the scriptural facts are all against it. The accounts of Matthew, Mark, Luke, and John show that that particular first day of the week was filled with confusion and unbelief, and that the disciples were not convinced of the resurrection until the first day at "even"—and this would be

Sunday night after the day was gone. In other words, it was actually the second day of the week.

Speaking of their state of mind on Sunday, Mark says: "They were affrighted." Mark 16:5. "They trembled and were amazed." Mark 16:8. "They were afraid." Mark 16:8. "They mourned and wept." Mark 16:10. "They . . . believed not." Mark 16:11. "Neither believed they them." Mark 16:13. Then after the close of the day, Jesus "upbraided them with their unbelief and hardness of heart, because they believed not them which had seen him after he was risen." Mark 16:14.

Luke says that on this day "they were much perplexed." Luke 24:4. "They were afraid." Luke 24:5. "Their words seemed . . . as idle tales, and they believed them not." Luke 24:11. "Ye walk, and are sad." Luke 24:17. "O fools, and slow of heart to believe." Luke 24:25. After the close of the day when Jesus appeared to them in the upper room, "they were terrified." "They were . . . affrighted, and supposed that they had seen a spirit." Luke 24:37. "They yet believed not." Luke 24:41.

John says it was that "same day" but "at evening" that they were in a room, and "the doors were shut . . . for fear of the Jews." Then Jesus came in where they were, and to dispel their unbelief, "shewed unto them his hands and his side." John 20:19, 20.

So these inspired men, writing later of the state of mind they were in during that day, reveal that they were as far from being in a state of joy and gladness as possible. Instead they were "affrighted," "amazed," "afraid," "perplexed," and "sad"; they "mourned," they "wept," they "believed not," they felt as though they were listening to "idle tales," they were "terrified," they were "slow of heart to believe," they "supposed that they had seen a spirit," etc. Such was their state of mind the whole day through, and it was not until evening that they were finally convinced of the resurrection of the Lord. It does seem that when men use such arguments, it would occur to them that some may read them or hear them who happened to be acquainted with the facts. How very scarce must be the evidence in favor of first-day observance when such farfetched and unscriptural arguments are used!

When David prophetically said, "This is the day which the Lord hath made; we will rejoice and be glad in it" (Psalm 118:24), he was looking ahead to the "day" when Christ would be on the earth. The Bible speaks of "the day of salvation" (2 Corinthians 6:2). Jesus said, "Your father Abraham rejoiced to see my day: and he saw it, and was glad." John

8:56. Here we have the words "rejoiced" and "glad" referring to the time of Christ. How many were made glad while He was here on earth? The eyes of the blind were opened; the ears of the deaf were unstopped; the lame were made to walk; the dead were raised to life. Jesus, Luke says, went "preaching . . . the glad tidings of the kingdom of God." Luke 8:1. Again Luke says, "All the people rejoiced for all the glorious things that were done." Luke 13:17. In Jesus' day there was continual rejoicing and gladness wherever He went. This is the day which David prophesied of, and not that day of confusion, sadness, and unbelief (on the part of the disciples) on which Jesus came forth from the dead. The Bible makes nothing of the *day* of Jesus' resurrection, but it makes much of the *fact* itself.

"The Lord's Day"

Some contend that the Lord's day of Revelation 1:10 is the first day of the week. Here the beloved John says, "I was in the Spirit on the Lord's day." He does not say it was the first day of the week. In fact the first day of the week is not mentioned in the book of Revelation. Now which day does the Bible teach is the Lord's day? Since Revelation 1:10 does not tell us which day it is, it will be necessary to search for this information in some other part of the Bible. We shall see that the Lord's day is the seventh-day Sabbath, and that it is the Lord's day for the same reason that we have the term "the Lord's Supper"—because the same Lord, the Son of God, is the author of both these divine institutions, and both are memorials of His work in behalf of the human race. The Lord's day is a memorial of the work of creation, and the Lord's Supper is the memorial of redemption. The work of creation was finished on the sixth day of the week, and then the Creator—the Son of God—rested from His wonderful works, which He "made . . . to be remembered." Then the same blessed Son of God some four thousand years later, near the close of the sixth day of the week, bowed His head and cried as He expired, "It is finished," and then rested again from His work on the Sabbath day in Joseph's new tomb.

How tired and weary He must have been! He was up all Thursday night and was hurried by the mob from one judgment to another; He was scourged cruelly; He was compelled to carry His cross until He fainted beneath the load; He was nailed to it and then was raised, and for some six hours He hung there. They took Him down and laid Him in Joseph's new tomb "wherein never man before was laid." It was immaculately clean and tidy. With His eyes closed, His hands folded over the pulseless heart of love, He rested—even as He had rested four thousand years before, through the sacred hours of the day which He Himself had blessed, sanctified, and hallowed for man. How sweet was His rest! It makes the Sabbath a memorial of the finished works of creation and the finished works of redemption, both accomplished by the same Lord. Surely it, and no other, is the Lord's day.

"Thus Saith the Lord"

That the Lord Jesus, the Son of God, was the One who actually did the work of creating the world in six days is further confirmed by the following words of Paul as he spoke of Christ: "For by him were all things created, that are in heaven, and that are in earth, visible and invisible, whether they be thrones, or dominions, or principalities, or powers: all things were created by him, and for him." Colossians 1:16. This certainly makes it plain that it was God's dear Son who created the world and all things therein in six days, and then "rested on the seventh day from all his work."

The Lord Himself declared, "The sabbath was made for man." Mark 2:27. This is the statement of a fact—"the sabbath was made." Now who made the Sabbath? Speaking of the Son of God, John says, "All things were made by him; and without him was not any thing made that was made." John 1:3.

Then "the sabbath was made," and "without him was not any thing made that was made." Again, "All things were created by him, and for him." Colossians 1:16. Then the Sabbath is the Lord's day because He made it.

The evidence that the Sabbath is the Lord's day seems exhaustless. Jesus Himself declared this fact when He said, "For the Son of man is Lord even of the sabbath day." Matthew 12:8.

Of which day does He declare Himself Lord? The Sabbath day. Then if He is Lord of the Sabbath day, does not that settle the fact that on Sabbath day is the Lord's day? The Lord's day is the day of which Christ is Lord, and He claimed to be Lord of the Sabbath day.

Notice how emphatically it is stated in Isaiah 58:13: "If thou turn away thy foot from the sabbath, from doing thy pleasure on my holy day." Here the Lord plainly calls the Sabbath His holy day.

Chapter 7

Origin of Sunday Observance

On the origin of Sunday observance, there is no better summarizing explanation than the words of Dr. Hiscox, author of *The Manual of the Baptist Churches*, and one of the best scholars the Baptists ever produced. In a talk before a Baptist ministers' convention in New York, he said:

"There was and is a commandment to keep holy the Sabbath day, but that Sabbath day was not Sunday. It will be said, however, and with some show of triumph, that the Sabbath was transferred from the seventh to the first day of the week, with all its duties, privileges, and sanctions. Earnestly desiring information on this subject, which I have studied for many years, I ask, Where is the record of such a transaction to be found? Not in the New Testament, absolutely not. There is no scriptural evidence of the change of the Sabbath institution from the seventh to the first day of the week.

"I wish to say that this Sabbath question, in this aspect of it, is the gravest and most perplexing question connected with Christian institutions which at this time claims attention from Christian people; and the only reason it is not a more disturbing element in Christian thought and religious discussions is because the Christian world has settled down content on the conviction that somehow a transference has taken place at the beginning of Christian history.

"To me it seems unaccountable that Jesus, during three years' intercourse with His disciples, often conversing with them upon the Sabbath question, discussing it in some of its various aspects, freeing it from its false glosses, never alluded to any transference of the day; also, that during forty days of His resurrection life, no such thing was intimated. Nor, so far as we know, did the Spirit which was given to bring to their remembrance all things whatsoever that He had said unto them deal with this question. Nor did the inspired apostles, in preaching the gospel, founding churches, counseling, and instructing those founded, discuss or approach this subject.

"Of course, I quite well know that Sunday did come into use in early Christian history as a religious day as we learn from the Christian fathers and other sources. But what a pity that it comes branded with the mark of paganism, and christened with the name of the sun god, when adopted and sanctioned by the papal apostasy, and bequeathed as a sacred legacy to Protestantism!"—The New York *Examiner*, November 16, 1893.

Now could admissions that there is no New Testament authority for keeping the first day of the week be more bold? Dr. Hiscox was a ripe student of the Scriptures and was never given to reckless statements. Every sentence uttered in this quotation shows deep thought and seriousness on his part. He simply states what Sabbathkeepers know, and what no one has ever disproved: that there is no New Testament authority for keeping the first day of the week.

Other Admissions

Sabbathkeepers are not alone in asserting that the New Testament does not teach the observance of the first day of the week. Some of the brightest scholars among Sundaykeepers happen to agree with them. In *Faith of Our Fathers*, by Cardinal Gibbons, are these words: "You may read the Bible from Genesis to Revelation , and you will not find a single line authorizing the sanctification of Sunday. The Scriptures enforce the observance of Saturday, a day which we never sanctify."—pg. 98.

In *Binney's Theological* Compend, which contains the doctrines of the Methodist Church, is this admission: "It is true there is no positive command for infant baptism, . . . nor is there any for keeping holy the first day of the week."

The editor of *The Christian at Work*, a Presbyterian paper, wrote in an editorial: "Some have tried to build the observance of Sunday upon apostolic command, whereas, the apostles gave no such command on the matter at all. . . . The truth is as soon as we appeal . . . to the Bible the Sabbatarians have the best of the arguments."

In a later edition this same Presbyterian paper said: "It is now seen, and is admitted, that we must go to later than apostolic times for the establishment of Sunday observance."

Any seventh-day observer will promise faithfully to abandon seventh-day keeping and will observe the first day of the week if anyone will fine one verse in all the Bible that say the first day of the week is the Lord's day; or one verse which says that Jesus or His disciples taught that the first day of the week was to take the place of the creation-Sabbath; one text that says Jesus or His disciples ever observed the first day of the week or ever commanded anyone else to do so; one text that says Christians or anyone else should not work on the first day of the week; then, finally, one text in all the Bible that says the Father, Son, Holy Spirit, angels, prophets, apostles, or inspired men ever, at any time, said one word about the first day of the week being in any sense a sacred day.

The Missing Text Still Missing

No one will ever produce the one text because it is not in the Bible. People keep the first day of the week because the apostate church in the early ages borrowed this custom from the heathen and handed it over to Protestantism. The heathen worshiped the sun on that day. Jesus said: "Howbeit in vain do they worship me, teaching for doctrines the commandments of men. For laying aside the commandment of God, ye hold the tradition of men." Mark 7:7, 8.

Sunday Christianized During Apostasy

Recall that Dr. Hiscox, after stating that there is no New Testament ground for Sunday observance, said: "Of course I quite well know that Sunday did come into use in early Christian history as a religious day as we learn from the Christian fathers and other sources. But what a pity that it comes branded with the mark of paganism, and christened with the name of the sun god, when adopted and sanctioned by the papal apostasy, and bequeathed as a sacred legacy to Protestantism!"

Dr. Hiscox's words "branded with the mark of paganism" mean that Sunday has always been the day of heathen worship. It has always been dedicated to the sun god, and that is what is meant by "christened with the name of the sun god." From the heathen practice of sun worship we get the word "Sunday." Speaking of the abominations being practiced in the time of Ezekiel, the prophet said, "And he brought me into the inner court of the Lord's house, and, behold, at the door of the temple of the Lord, between the porch and the altar, were about five and twenty men, . . . and their faces toward the east; and they worshiped the sun toward the east." Ezekiel 8:16.

The first day of the week was dedicated to the heavenly body that came first in importance, the sun, and hence the name. The second day of the week was dedicated to the moon and was called "moonday," from which we get Monday. Historical records show that Sunday was used as a day of worship ages before the resurrection of Christ. This is the background for the practice of worshiping on Sunday which was "adopted and sanctioned by the papal apostasy."

This apostasy developed very early. In Paul's day some held that the second coming of Christ was near at hand. The apostle in opposing this error wrote to the believers in Thessalonica:

"Let no man deceive you by any means: for that day shall not come, except there come a falling away first, and that man of sin be revealed, the son of perdition; who opposeth and exalteth himself above all that is called God, or that is worshipped; so that he as God sitteth in the temple of God, shewing himself that he is God. . . . And now ye know what withholdeth that he might be revealed in his time. For the mystery of iniquity doth already work: only he who now letteth will let, until he be taken out of the way. And then shall that Wicked be revealed, whom the Lord shall consume with the spirit of his mouth, and shall destroy with the brightness of his coming." 2 Thessalonians 2:3–8.

Summing this prophecy up, we find that some were teaching that the day of Christ was at hand. Paul said this was a deception because there would be first a falling away headed by the man of sin; that this man would sit in God's temple, accept worship, assume the place of God, etc. He said that as long as a certain personage whom Paul designated as *he* was not taken away, this mystery of iniquity which Paul said "doth already work" would be hindered; but as soon as the *he* was taken out of the way, this man of sin would be revealed, continue his apostate work through the ages, and be destroyed by the brightness of the Lord's coming. Paul based his conviction that the day of Christ was not at hand on the fact that this falling-away prophecy must be fulfilled first.

A.D.

"Son of Perdition"

Those who object to this man of sin being identified as the Papacy contend this cannot be true because the text speaks of a man called the son of perdition and refers to some superman and not a system. Let us note that the text speaks of the man of sin, the mystery of iniquity, the son of perdition, and "that Wicked" as being the same. It would seem to me that to confine these names to one man would be harder to accept than to say that these terms represent the principles functioning through the Roman Catholic Church. There is biblical backing for my assertion, too, for the word "son" in the singular is used to represent a complete nationalistic system. Speaking of Israel's (the twelve tribes') departure from Egypt, the Lord said, "And thou shalt say unto Pharaoh, Thus saith the Lord, Israel is my son, even my firstborn: and I say unto thee, Let my son go, that he may serve me."

Here Israel, the twelve tribes collectively, is called a son. So in 2 Thessalonians 2:3 the Romish system is spoken of as the "son of perdition" and "that man of sin." Since Paul said that this "mystery of iniquity" was already at work in his day, it will not surprise us to find that shortly after his death men began speaking perverse things and drawing disciples after them. By A.D. 330 the headquarters of the apostate church was firmly established in Rome.

Doubtful Authorities for Sunday-keepers

Now here is a strange thing. Sunday supporters, with a show of great triumph, quote Ignatius, Barnabas, Irenaeus, Clement, Tertullian, Augustine, and others to prove that first-day observance started *early*, because the writings of these men speak favorably of the first day of the week. Little do they realize that the Roman Catholics go to these same writings to prove doctrines which no other church in the world practices or believes today except the Roman Catholic Church. So instead of actually proving the first day is to keep, they are proving that the prophecy of Daniel 7:25 and the prophecy of Paul (that the falling away would develop more rapidly immediately following his departure) actually took place. The point is this: The testimony of these early fathers, instead of proving the first day is the day to keep, actually proves that it is not; it points out that Sunday-keeping was adopted from the heathen sun worshipers and is a counterfeit of the true Sabbath—and this counterfeit witnesses to the truth of Paul's prediction about the falling away.

I notice that all defenders of first-day observance quote Ignatius (A.D. 101) as favoring the first day instead of the seventh. I have before me Cardinal Gibbons' *Faith of Our Fathers*. I open the book to the chapter in which he is trying to prove that the priest turns the bread into God, and that this bread should be bowed to and worshiped as God. To prove this idolatry should be practiced, he quotes Ignatius condemning the people of his day "because they confess not that the Eucharist is the flesh of our Saviour Jesus Christ."—p. 297. There is no dogma that the Roman Catholic Church holds today more strongly than that the wafer over which the priest pronounces some Latin words is the actual Son of God. Such gross error leads me to conclude that the writings of Ignatius witness to the early "falling away" rather than that the first day is to be kept. The fact that he endorsed first-day observance is against it rather than for it—unless we are going to be Roman Catholics. (Those who quote these early Fathers neglect to inform their hearers that scholars have grave reason to doubt the authorship of these writings, especially those credited to Ignatius and Barnabas.)

Where are these writings of the early Fathers to be found? I have before me quite a large volume called *The Lost Books of the Bible*. The preface says these writings were "not included in the authorized New Testament." On page 172 of this book (which is filled with all sorts of follies and fables) I find "The Epistle of Ignatius to the Magnesians," and it is in this "epistle" that there is a statement favoring first-day keeping.

How few there are who, when this statement is quoted in books and pamphlets written in opposition to the Sabbath, know that it comes from *The Lost Books of the Bible*! Preachers will read from this book of fables with the same show of reverence and respect as though it were the Word of God.

Another early writer often quoted in favor of first-day observance is Barnabas. I find his writing on page 153 of *The Lost Books of the Bible*. I am ashamed to quote the things contained in these pages; I shall merely refer the reader to them, but at the same time I would be far more ashamed to read from such a source to prove first-day sacredness! Those ministers who quote from these sources know there is not one in a thousand who knows anything about the "Epistle of Barnabas," and they can take advantage of this ignorance to prove something which they cannot prove by the Bible!

Justin Martyr is another "authority" that is greatly relied upon to prove first-day sacredness. On page 297 of *Faith of Our Fathers* Cardinal Gibbons quotes Martyr to prove that the bread is Jesus Christ: "The Eucharist is both the flesh and blood of the same incarnate Jesus." Nobody believes that today except the Roman Catholics. All these "authorities" prove what Paul meant when he said that after his "departure," men would arise "speaking perverse things," and the fact that these writings (supposed to have been done by these men) are claimed to have been written right after the death of the apostles shows what Paul meant when he said, "The mystery of iniquity doth already work."

Clement of Alexandria is another one of the early Fathers. I find that he is another one whose writings go to make up *The Lost Books of the Bible.* He is supposed to have written his epistles one hundred years after the death of the last apostle. He says that by that time the seventh day had "become nothing more than a working day." Thus do we see that the church to which he belonged was gradually ceasing to observe the seventh day and leaning more and more toward the day of the sun. Just how reliable his writings are may be gathered from the following, which I dare to quote from him:

"There is a certain bird called Phoenix; of this there is never but one at a time; and that lives 500 years. And when the time of its dissolution draws near, that it must die, it makes itself a nest of frankincense, and myrrh, and other spices into which when its time is fulfilled it enters and dies. But its flesh putrefying, breeds a certain worm, which being nourished with the juice of the dead bird brings forth feathers; and when it is grown to a perfect state, it takes up the nest in which the bones of its parents lie, and carries it from Arabia into Egypt. And flying in open day in the sight of all men, lays it upon the altar of the sun, and so returns from whence it came."

Think about being compelled to read from such a source to prove Sunday had become the Sabbath! Note how he mentions the altar of the sun, from which comes sun-day and the observance of the first day of the week. No wonder he had come to recognize the seventh day as no more than a working day. How natural it was that as he turned from the true Sabbath, he leaned more and more to Sunday! At the risk of wearying the reader with further quotations from such writers as we are examining, I have two more to quote from. I quote from them because they are read with confidence in an effort to prove Sunday sacredness. One of these is Tertullian, and the other is Eusebius. Tertullian is supposed to have lived shortly after the death of the apostles.

Cardinal Gibbons relies to the utmost on Tertullian to prove some of the unscriptural Roman Catholic doctrines. On page 3 of *Faith of Our Fathers*, Gibbons says:

"It is also a very ancient and pious practice for the faithful to make on their person, the sign of the cross saying at the same time: 'In the name of the Father, and of the Son, and of the Holy Ghost.' Tertullian, who lived in the second century of the Christian era, says: 'In all our actions, when we come in or go out, when we dress and when we wash, at our meals, before retiring to sleep, we form on our foreheads the form of the cross. These practices are not commanded by a formal law of Scripture; but tradition teaches them, custom confirms them, faith observes them.' "

Roman Catholics practice these things today. Gibbons quotes Tertullian again: " 'The faithful wife will pray for the soul of her deceased husband, particularly on the anniversary day of his falling asleep. And if she fail to do so, she has repudiated her husband as far as it lies in her. " You see, Gibbons was trying to prove prayers for the dead. There is nothing in the Bible about this, so he goes to Tertullian. This is the same thing that is done trying to prove first-day keeping. If this man wrote what is attributed to him, he was certainly one of the builders of the Roman Catholic Church.

Eusebius, in A.D. 324, wrote, "We have transferred the duties of the Sabbath to Sunday." Who are the "we"? Certainly not the apostles. They could not do so after the testament was ratified by the death of the Testator on the cross. When Eusebius says, "We have transferred the duties of the Sabbath to Sunday," it reminds us again of what Paul foretold about those who, after his death, would speak "perverse things, to draw away disciples after them" (Acts 20:30). This last quotation from these early Fathers is dated A.D. 324. Just three years before, in 321, Constantine, half Christian and half pagan, made the first law to keep the "venerable day of the sun." Translated from the Latin, it reads: "Let all the judges and townspeople and the occupations of all trades rest upon the venerable day of the sun. But let those who are situated in the country, freely and at full liberty attend to the business of agriculture. Because it often happens that no other day is so fit for the sowing of corn or the planting of vines, lest the critical moment being let slip, men should lose the commodities of heaven. Given this 7th day of March, Crispus and Constantine being consuls each of them for the second time."

It will be noted that at that time working on Sunday was the general rule. It will be noticed that the day was not known by any sacred Christian title. It was called the venerable day of the sun. Thus do we see that little by little the true Sabbath was being discarded and Sunday was coming into recognition.

What the Catechism Says

Coming now to the Roman Catholic teachings, I quote the following questions and answers:

"Q. Which is the Sabbath day?

"A. Saturday is the Sabbath day.

"Q. Why do we observe Sunday instead of Saturday?

"A. We observe Sunday instead of Saturday because the Catholic Church, in the Council of Laodicea (A.D. 336), transferred the solemnity from Saturday to Sunday.

"Q. By what authority did the church substitute Sunday for Saturday?

"A. The church substituted Sunday for Saturday by the plenitude of that divine power which Christ bestowed upon her."—*The Convert's Catechism of Catholic Doctrine*, p. 50.

In claiming divine power to change the Ten Commandment law of God, the church fulfilled that prediction of Paul which said, "Shewing himself that he is God," and that of Daniel 7:25, which said, "He shall . . . think to change times and laws."

We have traced the steps, by was of the fulfillment of prophecy, by which the "falling away" came, giving birth in the organization known as the Roman Catholic Church. We have shown how the principles of error which were beginning to work in the days of Paul brought about the adoption of many heathen errors into the church. This brings us back to the truthfulness of Dr. Edward T. Hiscox's statement that was quoted at the beginning of this chapter.

"Of course I know quite well that Sunday did come into use in early Christian history as a religious day as we learn from the Fathers and other sources. But what a pity that it comes branded with the mark of paganism, and christened with the name of the sun god, when adopted and sanctioned by the papal apostasy, and bequeathed as a sacred legacy to Protestantism!"

Since many of the Romans who came into the apostate, or apostatizing, church were sun-worshipers before they came in, they were permitted to continue to give certain respect to that day, but were instructed that its observance should have to do with the risen Son rather than the rising sun. Gradually as the pagan element grew into influence and power in the church, the true Sabbath was practically supplanted by Sunday.

Thus was Sunday "adopted and sanctioned by the papal apostasy," and at the time of the Reformation it was "bequeathed as a sacred legacy to Protestantism." These are the facts with reference to the origin of Sunday observance. Its observance has not the remotest relation to the resurrection. In order to overcome the idolatrous "flavor" of the day it was clothed with the sentiment of the resurrection. In Matthew 15:13 Jesus said, "Every plant, which my heavenly Father hath not planted, shall be rooted up." We herewith have shown that the seventh day is of divine planting and eternally rooted in the writings of the Old and New Testaments. What about Sunday? We find that it is rooted deeply in the fertile soil of sun-worshiping heathenism and idolatrous practices.

Suppose you were requested to supply the following texts, what would they be?

1. In Matthew 26:26–28 we read about Jesus' instituting the Lord's Supper, how it should be observed, and what it stood for. If you were asked to give texts which tell about Jesus' instituting the observance of the first day of the week in memory of the resurrection, how it should be observed in language just as definite as that used when He instituted the Lord's Supper, which texts would you give?

Texts . . . .

2. If you were requested to give a text which says the first day of the week is the Lord's day, which text would you give?

Text . . . .

3. In Romans 4:15 we read that "where no law is, there is no transgression," and in 5:13, "but sin is not imputed when there is no law." If you were asked for texts saying it is a sin to work on the first day of the week, which texts would you give?

Texts . . . .

4. Since Mark 1:32 says that evening came "when the sun did set," and since Luke 24:29 says that "the day is far spent" when it is "toward evening," the day is entirely "spent" when the sun sets. If you were requested to give a text which says the first day of the week begins six hours after sunset and ends six hours after sunset, which texts would you give?

Texts . . . .

"Thy word is truth." "The scripture cannot be broken."

Chapter 8

What Was Abolished at the Cross?

Many of the commandments of the Old Testament enjoined the practicing of ceremonies which were intended to cease at the cross because they pointed ahead to the death of Christ. To practice these things after the death of Christ would be in fact denying His death. The Ten Commandments are entirely different in their meaning and duration; for God never intended that the time would come when the law against stealing, lying, killing, etc. would be abolished. I have often been asked, "If you are going to observe the seventh day, why don't you offer sacrifices?" Such a question reveals a superficial concept of the Bible teachings. It would be just as logical to ask, "If you are going to observe the commandment which says, 'Thou shalt not take the name of the Lord thy God in vain,' why not offer the sacrifices?"

This chapter is being written to prove what a vast difference there is between the law of the Ten Commandments and the ceremonial law, why one was done away at the cross and the other was not.

Two Laws in the Old Testament

If the honest-hearted reader can understand once and for all that there were two laws in the Old Testament—the law of sacrifices, which was abolished, and another, the law of the Ten Commandments, which was not abolished—it will then be easily understood why Christians should observe the seventh day but should not offer the sacrifices. Then when we read in the New Testament about a law which was abolished at the cross, we will not become confused, thinking it is the law of the Ten Commandments. That there are two laws, one of which was abolished, whereas the other was not, will be plain from the reading of the following texts:

"Having abolished in his flesh the enmity, even the law of commandments contained in ordinances." Ephesians 2:15.

"For the priesthood being changed, there is made of necessity a change also of the law." Hebrews 7:12.

"Blotting out the handwriting of ordinances that was against us, which was contrary to us, and took it out of the way, nailing it to the cross." Colossians 2:14.

That there was in addition to this abolished law another law that was not abolished the following texts prove beyond controversy:

"And it is easier for heaven and earth to pass, than one tittle of the law to fail." Luke 16:17.

"Do we then make void the law through faith? God forbid: yea, we establish the law." Romans 3:31.

"For whosoever shall keep the whole law, and yet offend in one point, he is guilty of all." James 2:10.

If we hold that there were not two laws, we have the first three of these scriptures contradicting the other three. If the reader will turn to Exodus 19:16–18, he will find why this is true.

"It came to pass on the third day in the morning, that there were thunders and lightnings, and a thick cloud upon the mount, and the voice of the trumpet exceeding loud; so that all the people that was in the camp trembled. And Moses brought forth the people out of the camp to meet with God; and they stood at the nether part of the mount. And mount Sinai was altogether on a smoke, because the Lord descended upon it in fire."

Then as the people listened in silence and awe, they heard distinctly the voice of the Lord saying:

1. "Thou shalt have no other gods before me.

2. "Thou shalt not make unto thee any graven image, or any likeness of any thing that is the heaven above, or that is in the earth beneath, or that is in the water under the earth: thou shalt not bow down thyself to them, nor serve them: for I the Lord thy God am a jealous God, visiting the iniquity of the fathers upon the children unto the third and fourth generation of them that hate me, and shewing mercy unto thousands of them that love me, and keep my commandments.

3. "Thou shalt not take the name of the Lord thy God in vain; for the Lord will not hold him guiltless that taketh his name in vain.

4. "Remember the sabbath day, to keep it holy. Six days shalt thou labour, and do all thy work: but the seventh day is the sabbath of the Lord thy God: in it thou shalt not do any work, thou, nor thy son, nor thy daughter, thy manservant, nor thy maidservant, nor thy cattle, nor thy

stranger that is within thy gates: for in six days the Lord made heaven and earth, the sea, and all that in them is, and rested the seventh day: wherefore the Lord blessed the sabbath day, and hallowed it.

5. "Honour thy father and thy mother: that thy days may be long upon the land which the Lord thy God giveth thee.

6. "Thou shalt not kill.

7. "Thou shalt not commit adultery.

8. "Thou shalt not steal.

9. "Thou shalt not bear false witness against thy neighbor.

10. "Thou shalt not covet thy neighbour's house, thou shalt not covet thy neighbours' wife, nor his manservant, nor his maidservant, nor his ox, nor his ass, nor any thing that is thy neighbour's." Exodus 20:3–17.

The Bible calls these "the ten commandments." In proof of this we read the following verses:

"And he wrote upon the tables the words of the covenant, the ten commandments." Exodus 34:28.

"And he declared unto you his covenant, which he commanded you to perform, even ten commandments." Deuteronomy 4:13.

"And he wrote on the tables, according to the first writing, the ten commandments." Deuteronomy 10:4.

The Decalogue

If all the other commandments were to be counted with these, there would certainly be more than ten. The word "ten" limits the number. That God never intended that any other commandments be added to these, thus making more than ten, is plainly proved by Deuteronomy 5:22: "These words the Lord spake . . . and he added no more." If God added no more to these ten, where is the man who has authority to add the multiplicity of sacrificial laws and yearly sabbaths to these commandments? God made the week out of seven days. That fixed the number of days of the week. What man has authority to add other days to the seven and claim that the week has ten, twenty, a hundred, or even more days in it? When God said "seven," He limited the week to that number of days, and it cannot be changed. Then when God said "ten commandments" and "added no more," how can man say that the law contained hundreds of commandments? The week cannot have as many as eight days in it, and the Decalogue does not have as many as eleven commandments in it. The fact that the Lord used the word "ten" shows that none of the other commandments are to be counted into this law.

When, in Daniel 7:7, Daniel declared that the fourth beast had ten horns, can man change that fact and make it more than what God said? When verse twenty-four of the same chapter says, "The ten horns out of this kingdom are ten kings that shall arise," can man add to these and prove there were more than ten? Cannot we see that "ten" limits the number? When God says ten commandments are in the law, can man change the number "ten" to include the scores of other commandments found scattered here and there in the five books of Moses? Yet that is the very thing men try to do in order to include the Ten Commandments in the "law of commandments contained in ordinances," which was abolished. Such should remember God's Word says, "Add thou not unto his words, lest he reprove thee, and thou be found a liar." Proverbs 30:6.

After having spoken the Decalogue, the Lord wrote it on two tables of stone, indicating the immutability of the principles it contained. Notice, too, that these Ten Commandments which the Lord spoke and wrote are called a law and not just a small part of a law: "Come up to me into the mount, and be there: and I will give thee tables of stone, and a law, and commandments which I have written." Exodus 24:12. Here we are told that that which the Lord wrote on tables of stone is a law. What did He write on tables of stone? We read: "And he wrote on the tables . . . the ten commandments, which the Lord spake unto you in the mount out of the midst of the fire in the day of the assembly." Deuteronomy 10:4. If this language does not prove that the Ten Commandments constituted a complete law, composed of a certain number of commandments to which were to be added no more, then language has no meaning.

This is the law in which the Lord says, "Remember the sabbath day, to keep it holy"; and because it says this, *and for no other reason*, it is being claimed today that it was abolished. A standard reference book defines the word "abolish" to mean "to do away with; put an end to; annul; destroy; abrogate, annihilate, end, eradicate, exterminate, obliterate, overthrow, remove, revoke, set aside, stamp out, terminate." This is what is claimed by no-law teachers to have happened to the commandments which instruct the children to honor their parents, which enjoin purity of life, honesty, truthfulness, reverence for the Lord's name and His holy day, etc. When we come to think about just what this law teaches, it is hard to understand how any normal mind can argue that it was abolished.

James and the Law

The fact that the death of Jesus never set aside a single one of the prohibitions of the Ten Commandment law, together with the fact that anyone who willfully violates one of the commandments of this law is accounted guilty before God, is abundantly proved by James 2:10: "For whosoever shall keep the whole law, and yet offend in one point, he is guilty of all."

The next verse proves the law referred to is the law of Ten Commandments. Get your Bible and read: "For he [that law, margin] that said, Do not commit adultery, said also, Do not kill. Now if thou commit no adultery, yet if thou kill, thou art become a transgressor of the law."

These texts cannot be passed by lightly. They stand opposed to the claim that the law of Ten Commandments was not complete and separate. When this apostle spoke of the whole law, he did not have his mind on the entire five books of Moses. He was quoting the Ten Commandments. He declares the whole of that law is to be obeyed. This is the same law which says, "The seventh day is the sabbath of the Lord thy God."

Suppose it were contended that if a man practices lying, theft, immorality, or violates any one of the commandments (except the fourth), he will be lost. No one would argue about it. But when the same man is confronted with the application of James' words to the Sabbath commandment, he will not have it that way. But it is there in God's Word, and the refusal to accept it does not alter it in the least.

Suppose James 2:11 read: "For that law which said, Do not commit adultery, said also, Bring a lamb of the first year for an offering. Now if thou commit no adultery, yet if thou bring not the lamb, thou art become a transgressor of the law." That would sound strange, would it not? It would be mixing the two laws. According to the argument that there are not two laws, this reading would be in perfect accord with the Bible. But since James quotes two of the Ten Commandments to illustrate his point, it proves that he had reference to the Decalogue; and when he says the whole of that law is to be obeyed, it is certain that the Ten Commandment law, as a whole, is still to be respected and obeyed.

Those who hold that all the Ten Commandments were abolished at the cross and then later almost all were brought back to life "and incorporated into the grace system" purposely avoid James 2:10. It says "the whole law," and they say, "No, not the whole law—the Sabbath was dropped out at the cross." James was discussing the truth that justification by faith does not give license to transgress the law. He says (James 2:14): "What doth it profit, my brethren, though a man say he hath faith, and have not works? Can faith save him?" Then he goes on to say: "Even so faith, if it hath not works, is dead, being alone. Yea, a man may say, Thou hast faith, and I have works; shew me thy faith without thy works, and I will shew thee my faith by my works. . . . But wilt thou know, O vain man, that faith without works is dead?" Verses 17–20.

In the face of these verses, which James used to explain what he meant when he said, "Whosoever shall keep the whole law, and yet offend in one point, he is guilty of all," how can an honest man wrest what James says to mean that his topic was condemning justification by works? He was condemning the error of the dispensationalists in their claim that obedience is an impossibility, and that the doctrine of justification by faith gives license to transgress God's holy law. God, through Christ, has made provision for obedience to the Ten Commandments. In Revelation 12:17 we read of a "remnant . . . which keep the commandments of God." God says they do, so that disproves the contention that even God cannot enable anyone to keep them. Then Revelation 14:12 says, "Here are they that keep the commandments of God." There will be such a people, or God would not say so.

"The Law of Liberty"

James speaks of the Decalogue as "the law of liberty." It is such to those who are led by the Holy Spirit, for that Spirit kills the love for sin. The same law is an instrument of restraint to the man whose "carnal mind" wishes to transgress it. The law against the sale of narcotics is a restraint to the man who is a dope fiend. To the man who is not, it is a law of liberty. The law which says, "The seventh day is the sabbath," is a law of liberty to the man who loves the Sabbath and the principles for which it stands. It is not to the man who wishes to desecrate the Sabbath. Such a person tries to do away with the law. What he should do is pray that the Lord will take away the "carnal mind" which "is not subject to the law of God, neither indeed can be" (Romans 8:7).

We have proved that the whole law of the Ten Commandments is to be obeyed, and that if a man willfully breaks one point and practices that violation, he is guilty of all. He cannot satisfy ten points of requirements with nine points of obedience.

Not to Destroy but to Fulfill

In the Sermon on the Mount Jesus declared: "Think not that I am come to destroy the law, or the prophets: I am not come to destroy, but to fulfill. For verily I say unto you, Till heaven and earth pass, one jot or one tittle shall in no wise pass from the law, till all be fulfilled." Then in view of this Jesus added: "Whosoever therefore shall break one of these least commandments, and shall teach men so, he shall be called the least in the kingdom of heaven: but whosoever shall do and teach them, the same shall be called great in the kingdom of heaven." Matthew 5:17–19.

The fact that Jesus fulfilled the law does not mean that He ended it, but that He kept it as an example to us. The same Jesus came "to fulfil all righteousness," which includes baptism (Matthew 3:14, 15). Did Jesus do away with the law of baptism? The only way to fulfill duties based on love to God and love to man is to live out these duties in the life, and that is exactly what Jesus did. And "he that saith he abideth in him ought himself also so to walk, even as he walked." 1 John 2:6.

Two Laws

When Paul said to the Gentile Christians at Rome so emphatically, "Do we then make void the law through faith? God forbid: yea, we establish the law" (Romans 3:31), he had reference to the immutable law of Ten Commandments. But there was another law besides this one. The Lord did not speak it directly to the people with His own voice; He never wrote it on tables of stone; He never had it placed in the ark. This law was abolished at the cross. This is the law, as we shall see, that Paul refers to when he mentions Christ as "having abolished in his flesh . . . the law of commandments contained in ordinances" (Ephesians 2:15).

We will now proceed to discover this other law—what is contained in it, and why it came to an end at the cross.

The two laws—the Ten Commandment law that was not abolished, and the other law that was abolished—are spoken of in Deuteronomy 33:1, 2: "This is the blessing, wherewith Moses the man of God blessed the children of Israel before his death. And he said, "The Lord came from Sinai, and rose up from Seir unto them; he shined forth from mount Paran, and he came with ten thousands of saints: from his right hand went a fiery law for them."

Here we are definitely told that that which the Lord proclaimed to the people on Sinai was "a fiery law"—not part of a law, but "a . . . law." Then in verse four we read, "Moses commanded us a law, even the inheritance of the congregation of Jacob." It is plain that the Lord commanded a law and that Moses commanded a law. This certainly makes two laws. In Deuteronomy 4:11–14 we have both these laws plainly mentioned.

"Ye came near and stood under the mountain; and the mountain burned with fire unto the midst of heaven, with darkness, clouds, and thick darkness. And the Lord spake unto you out of the midst of the fire: ye heard the voice of the words, but saw no similitude; only ye heard a voice. And he declared unto you his covenant, which he commanded you to perform, even ten commandments; and he wrote them upon two tables of stone. And the Lord commanded me at that time to teach you statutes and judgments, that ye might do them in the land whither ye go over to possess it."

Here we have it. The Lord commanded a law of Ten Commandments and wrote them and "no more" (Deuteronomy 5:22) on tables of stone. That was one law. At the same time He told Moses to command them statutes, and this made another law; for Deuteronomy 33:4 says, "Moses commanded us a law." Nothing could be plainer. The Lord commanded a law, and Moses commanded a law. One and one equals two.

Speaking of this hundreds of years later in 2 King 21:8, God said: "Neither will I make the feet of Israel move any more out of the land which I gave their fathers; only if they will observe to do according to all that I have commanded them, and according to all the law that my servant Moses commanded them."

Here we read that that which Moses commanded was a law. Then we have read in a number of places that that which the Lord commanded and wrote on two tables of stone is a law. Certainly Inspiration recognizes that there were two laws. What I am contending is that there was a difference in the way in which they were given; one was spoken by the Lord with His own voice to the people, and the Lord told Moses to command the other. That which the Lord commanded was written on the two tables of stone, and that which Moses commanded was not. The law which the Lord spoke and then wrote with His finger on tables of stone was placed in the ark; the other law was not. The law which the Lord commanded and wrote on tables of stone was to abide till heaven and earth pass away (Luke 16:17). The other was typical and ceremonial and was "abolished in his flesh" on the cross (Ephesians 2:15). Plainly there were two laws.

Moses' Law of Ceremonies

Now let us see some things that were in the law which Moses commanded the people, and why it passed away at the cross. We turn to Leviticus 4:1–4:

"The Lord spake unto Moses, saying, Speak unto the children of Israel, saying, If a soul shall sin through ignorance against any of the commandments of the Lord concerning things which ought not to be done, and shall do against any of them: . . . then let him bring for his sin, which he hath sinned, a young bullock without blemish unto the Lord for a sin offering. And he shall bring the bullock unto the door of the tabernacle of the congregation before the Lord; and shall lay his hand upon the bullock's head, and kill the bullock before the Lord."

What did this mean? Let us say that a man had sinned and brought upon himself the sentence of death. (The bullock had not sinned.) The man placed his hand upon the bullock's head and transferred the guilt from himself to this substitute. Then, with his own hand, he took the life of the animal, thus admitting that he ought to die but that a substitute died in his stead. So it is with us and Christ. We have sinned, and because of this "death passed upon all men." Our sins were laid upon Jesus, and He died in our stead. The animal sacrifice provided a way for a man to express his belief that someday God would send the Lamb of God to die as his substitute.

The day before Jesus died, a man conscious of guilt was under obligation to sacrifice an animal as an expression of his faith that God would send His Son to die as a substitute. But the next day after Jesus died, it was not proper to kill the animal, because to do so would be to deny Jesus had died. In the book of Hebrews we read: "Neither by the blood of goats and calves, but by his own blood he entered in once into the holy place, having obtained eternal redemption for us." Hebrews 9:12.

Since Jesus' death we no longer bring an animal sacrifice for sin. We can see that this regulation came to an end at the cross, but it was no part of the law of the Ten Commandments. It was in the law of types and foreshadowed the death of the Lamb of God; and when that event occurred, the law of sacrifices ceased. Not so with the Sabbath. See Luke 23:56.

Before going further, we should understand this fact: The death of the animal canceled the sentence, but it did not cancel the law which imposed the sentence. Suppose the sin of the man was theft. He made confession of the sin, and the animal died in his stead. Did the law against theft die, too? Could he then go and steal anything he wished? Let us make the application to the death of Christ. Did Christ's death abolish the sentence or the law—which? When the lamb died, did the law the man had transgressed die, too? When Christ died, did the law which man had transgressed die, too? Can we not see the point? Do we not see how impossible it would be for the law to die, too?

Then another thing: This man came with his sacrifice to the sanctuary. As he walked along, he was "under the law"—under its condemnation. After his sacrifice was offered and he was pardoned, he went away "under grace." Did this grace give him license to keep on stealing? God forbid.

Two Kinds of Sabbaths

The law which Moses commanded enjoined the observance of a number of yearly sabbaths, as Leviticus 23:4–7 reveals.

"These are the feasts of the Lord, even holy convocations, which ye shall proclaim in their seasons. In the fourteenth day of the first month at even is the Lord's passover. And on the fifteenth day of the same month is the feast of unleavened bread unto the Lord: seven days ye must eat unleavened bread. In the first day [of the seven beginning on the fifteenth day of the month] ye shall have an holy convocation: ye shall do no servile work therein."

Here we have one of the yearly sabbaths. It came once a year on the fifteenth day of the first month. That being the case, it came on a different day of the week year by year just as does the Fourth of July. The first day of the seventh month of every year was also a sabbath. We read in verses twenty-three and twenty-four: "And the Lord spake unto Moses, saying, Speak unto the children of Israel, saying, In the seventh month, in the first day of the month, shall ye have a sabbath, a memorial of blowing of trumpets, an holy convocation." Note that this is not a weekly Sabbath. It came on the first day of the seventh month every year.

We read in verses twenty-six to twenty-eight that the tenth day of the seventh month was always observed as a rest day: "And the Lord spake unto Moses, saying, Also on the tenth day of this seventh month there shall be a day of atonement: . . . and ye shall afflict your souls, and offer an offering made by fire unto the Lord. And ye shall do no work in that same day."

In verses thirty-three and thirty-five we read that the fifteenth day of this seventh month was a rest day: "The Lord spake unto Moses, saying, Speak unto the children of Israel, saying, The fifteenth day of this seventh month shall be the feast of tabernacles for seven days unto the Lord. On the first day shall be an holy convocation: ye shall do no servile work therein."

Thus we have discovered four yearly sabbaths that were not in the Ten Commandment law. They are as follows:

1. The fifteenth day of the first month.
2. The first day of the seventh month.
3. The tenth day of the seventh month.
4. The fifteenth day of the seventh month.

There were other yearly sabbaths besides these. Then there were months and times and years and new moons that were to be observed in special ways. All these were in the law which the Lord told Moses to give to the people; they were not in the Ten Commandment law.

Summing up these yearly sabbaths and mentioning the distinction between them and the weekly seventh-day Sabbath, we find in Leviticus 23:37, 38: "These are the feasts of the Lord, which he shall proclaim to be holy convocations, to offer an offering made by fire unto the Lord, a burnt offering, and a meat offering, a sacrifice, and drink offerings, every thing upon his day: beside the sabbaths of the Lord."

Notice how the Holy Spirit makes plain the distinction between the yearly sabbaths and the weekly Sabbath. The yearly sabbaths were to be observed "beside the sabbaths of the Lord." We read in the fourth commandment that "the seventh day is the sabbath of the Lord." This Sabbath, or "rest of the Lord," was in the Ten Commandment law. The others were not. They were not the sabbaths of the Lord because He never rested on these days. But at the close of creation week He did rest on the seventh day from all His work. This makes it the Sabbath of the Lord. Thus do we see a vast difference.

When some read in the New Testament about sabbath days that were shadows of the body of Christ and that passed away at the cross, they become confused and declare they mean the weekly Sabbath. They do greatly err and lead many uninformed people into error. Let us turn to Colossians 2:14–17 and read about the abolition of these sabbath days that were in the law and that enjoined meat offerings, drink offerings, new moons, and festivals.

"Blotting out the handwriting of ordinances that was against us, which was contrary to us, and took it out of the way, nailing it to his cross; . . . let no man therefore judge you in meat, or in drink, or in respect of a holyday [a feast day, A.S.V.], or of the new moon, or of the sabbath days, which are a shadow of things to come; but the body is of Christ."

There was nothing in the Ten Commandment law about meats, drinks, new moons, sabbath days (plural), or feast days. All these were in the law which the Lord told Moses to command to the people. The weekly Sabbath is not mentioned in these texts. Paul says plainly that he is speaking of "sabbath days which are a shadow of things to come," and not of the weekly Sabbath which was a memorial of something that happened in the past at creation.

The fourth commandment does not tell us to keep the seventh day as a type of something to come. It says: "Remember the sabbath day, to keep it holy. . . . For in six days the Lord made heaven and earth, the sea, and all that in them is, and rested the seventh day: wherefore the Lord blessed the sabbath day, and hallowed it."

There is all the difference in the world between a typical shadow and a memorial. A shadow points forward, and a memorial points backward. The contrast is as distinct as that between night and day. And to show that He never had the weekly Sabbath in mind, the Holy Spirit distinctly mentioned "sabbath days which are a shadow of things to come." Of course the word "days" in this text (Colossians 2:14–17) is supplied, but this is justified by the fact that the word "sabbath" in the Greek is in the plural. Anyone may confirm this by consulting any Greek lexicon.

The King James Version uses the word "holyday," and some may contend that it means "the weekly Sabbath" and the expression "sabbath days" means "the yearly sabbaths." The American Standard Version uses "feast day" instead of "holyday." This is correct. For the word translated "holyday" here is from the Greek *heorte*, and in John 5:1 this word is used to designate one of the yearly festivals of the Jews: "After this there was a feast [*heorte*] of the Jews; and Jesus went up to Jerusalem."

This is one of the holy days that Paul spoke of as having been abolished. Thus do the evidences multiply that it is absolutely wrong to tell people that these verses prove that the weekly Sabbath was abolished. We should further observe that "shadows" pointed to Jesus as a Saviour from sin and were observed with that in mind. But the weekly Sabbath was made for man before sin ever entered into the world. The shadows pointing forward to His death as an atonement for sin certainly were not instituted until after sin. But the Lord's rest day existed before man needed atoning blood to save him from his guilt. Now since the weekly Sabbath was instituted before sin, just as was the marriage institution, it was not a shadow of Christ's death as a Saviour from sin; and His death never brought it to an end any more than it brought the marriage institution to an end. Both institutions came to us from the sinless Garden of Eden.

Paul's very language to the Christians at Colosse proves he had reference to the shadowy ceremonies which pointed forward to and ended at the cross. Notice carefully his words in Colossians 2:14: "Blotting out the handwriting of ordinances that was against us, which was contrary to us, and took it out of the way, nailing it to his cross."

As plain as he can make it, Paul declares they were "ordinances" that were nailed to the cross. They were ordinances that would be "contrary" to the faith of Christians to observe. In fact he declares that the observance of these would be "against us." Now for the use of some good common sense. Would it be contrary to Christian faith and practice and against Christian principle to refrain from idolatry, profanity, Sabbath desecration, dishonoring parents, murder, theft, adultery, lying, and coveting? How could it be "contrary" to Christian principle and "against us" to refrain from the immoralities and vices condemned by the Ten Commandments? How unreasonable to think that Paul was arguing thus! He was talking of another law which enjoined meat offerings, drink offerings, the observance of feasts, new moons, and yearly sabbaths.

Ceremonies Cease at Calvary

Why would the observance of these ceremonies after the death of Christ be contrary to Christian faith and teachings? The answer is easy. Take the Passover sabbath that came during the first month every year. The killing of the Passover lamb typified the death of the Lamb of God. To offer it after His death would be saying, in figure, that Jesus had not died. It would be a repudiation of His death and atoning blood. Surely such an observance would be contrary to the teachings of Christianity. The apostle Paul declares, "For even Christ our passover is sacrificed for us." 1 Corinthians 5:7. All the other typical ordinances in this law pointed to the death of Jesus on the cross, too. All these feasts, meat and drink offerings, and sabbaths that were nailed to the cross, Paul declares, were "a shadow of things to come"; and then he adds, "But the body is of Christ." That is, the body, or substance, that casts these shadows was Christ's body on the cross.

Now even a child knows that late in the afternoon when a tall tree casts its shadow eastward, one can begin at the farthest end of the shadow and follow it until he gets to the tree, or body, that casts it, and there it ceases. Just so, we may go back to the time when "by one man [Adam] sin entered into the world, and death by sin," and there a merciful God promised to send a Redeemer (Genesis 3:15), a Substitute, to die in man's place. To keep man continually reminded of this fact and to supply him with a means of expressing his faith in the coming sacrifice, God instituted these ceremonies. Most of them were given to man immediately after the fall; later several others were added, and all were included in the law which was not written on tables of stone.

Follow these shadowy ceremonies all the way from Eden to the time of Moses, and from then through the wilderness journey, and then on for hundreds of years after the settlement of Canaan, and at last to Calvary; there they cease. So it would be "against us" and "contrary" to our faith to observe these ceremonies after Jesus' death. To do so would be to deny that He had died. Not so with the other law. It is just as necessary to refrain from idolatry, profanity, Sabbath desecration, murder, adultery, and theft after the cross as before. In fact it was the violation of these principles that caused the death of Christ. Could they have been set aside or changed to accommodate the carnal mind, Jesus need not have died.

Now with these truths before us, let us again read Colossians 2:14–17 and see how plainly Paul reveals that he had no reference to the Ten Commandments.

"Blotting out the handwriting of ordinances that was against us, which was contrary to us, and took it out of the way, nailing it to his cross; and having spoiled principalities and powers, he made a shew of them openly, triumphing over them in it. Let no man therefore judge you in meat, or in drink, or in respect of an holyday, or of the new moon, or of the sabbath days: which are a shadow of things to come; but the body is of Christ."

The Testimony of Scholarship

How plain it is that not one of the Ten Commandments is mentioned or even hinted at. Albert Barnes, one of the most noted Presbyterian commentators of our country, reinforces this fact in his commentary on the New Testament.

"The allusion here is to the festivals of the Jews. . . . There is not the slightest reason to believe that he meant to teach that one of the Ten Commandments had ceased to be binding on mankind. If he had used the word in the singular number—'THE Sabbath'—it would then, of course, have been clear that he meant to teach that that commandment had ceased to be binding. . . . But the use of the term in the plural number, and the connection, show that he had his eye on the greater number of days which were observed by the Hebrews as festivals. . . . No part of the moral law—no one of the Ten Commandments—could be spoken of as '*a shadow* of good things to come.' These commandments are, from the nature of moral law, of perpetual and universal obligation."

Albert Barnes was versed in Latin, Hebrew, and Greek. He had no prejudices against people who observe the Sabbath. He was one of the best informed scholars the Presbyterian Church ever produced, and he declares that Colossians 2:14–17 has no reference to the abolition of the weekly Sabbath or any of the Ten Commandments. He agrees with Paul that it was "sabbath days which are a shadow of things to come" that were abolished, and not the memorial-of-the-creation Sabbath.

If this Ten Commandment law did not declare, "The seventh day is the sabbath of the Lord thy God," none would find fault with it. But in order to get rid of the Sabbath, it is necessary to do away with the entire law. There is no other way out. The Sabbath is a part of this law which forbids murder, theft, adultery, etc. As long as this law abides, the Sabbath must also because it is part of this law.

Dwight L. Moody, founder of the Moody Bible Institute, says: "The people must be made to understand that the Ten Commandments are still binding, and that there is a penalty attached to their violation. We do not want a gospel of mere sentiment. The Sermon on the Mount did not blot out the Ten Commandments."—*Weighed and Wanting*, p. 16.

Dr. C. I. Scofield, in his pamphlet "Rightly Dividing the Word of Truth," positively declares that Colossians 2:14–17 has reference to the ceremonial law only.

Adam Clarke, the Methodist commentator, when he reached Colossians 2:14–17, took the same stand as did Albert Barnes, namely, that Paul had not the remotest thought of the Ten Commandments. He says: "The apostle speaks here in reference to some particulars of the *hand-writing of ordinances*, which had been *taken away*, . . . the necessity of observing certain *holidays* or *festivals*; such as the *new moons* and particular *sabbaths*, . . . all these had been taken out of the way, and nailed to the cross, and were no longer of moral obligation. There is no intimation here that the Sabbath was done away or that its moral use was superseded, by the introduction of Christianity. I have shown elsewhere, that *remember the sabbath day, to keep it holy*, is a commandment of *perpetual obligation*."

It will be of interest just here to quote from the founder of the Methodist Church, John Wesley.

"But the moral law contained in the Ten Commandments, and enforced by the prophets, He did not take away. It was not the design of His coming to revoke any part of this. This is a law which never can be broken, which 'stands fast as the faithful witness in heaven.' The moral stands on an entirely different foundation from the ceremonial or ritual law."—*Sermons*, Vol. 1, pp. 221, 222.

Distinguishing Between the Laws

The following illustration will thoroughly convince the honest in heart that the law of Ten Commandments was a distinct and separate law, and that when the other "law of commandments contained in ordinances" (Ephesians 2:15) was abolished, the Ten Commandments were not included.

We may go over every one of the Ten Commandments and agree that on the day before Jesus died, it was sin to willfully have other gods, worship images, and desecrate the Lord's name and the Lord's Sabbath day; and we may agree that on the day before Jesus died, it was sin to willfully violate the commandments which forbid disrespect for parents, murder, adultery, theft, lying, and coveting. Now we ask in all sincerity: Was it sin to violate these same commandments the next day after Jesus died? Was it not just as wicked to steal, lie, and kill the day after Jesus died as the day before? Not if these commandments were all abolished at Calvary.

Let us now put the commandments in the other law to the same test and see what we find. The day before Jesus died it was obligatory to celebrate the Passover and the Passover sabbath; if a man committed a sin, he was under obligation to bring a lamb without spot or blemish for a sin offering; infants were to be circumcised. Were the commandments which enjoined these things in force the next day after Jesus died? Would the disciples have been held guilty of sin if they had ignored these ordi-

nances the next day after Jesus died? Most assuredly not. Thus do we see that these commandments were not of the same durability as were the ten.

Another very important distinction between the Ten Commandments and all the others is the fact that the Ten Commandments were placed inside the ark; and the others, in the side of the ark. In Deuteronomy 10:5 we read concerning the Decalogue: "I turned myself and came down from the mount, and put the tables in the ark which I had made; and there they be, as the Lord commanded me." Deuteronomy 31:26 tells where the other law was placed: "Take this book of the law, put it in the side of the ark of the covenant of the Lord your God." Here we have one law "in the ark," and the other "in the side of the ark."

There is a reason why the Ten Commandments were placed inside the ark, and it must not be overlooked. The ark was the most sacred article in the temple. It was placed in the holy of holies, and over it were cherubim (angels) of glory (Hebrews 9:5). It was from the mercy seat that mercy and grace were dispensed to the penitent transgressor. Of the angels at the ends of the ark it was written: "The cherubims shall stretch forth their wings on high, covering the mercy seat with their wings, and their faces shall look one to another; toward the mercy seat shall the faces of the cherubims be." Exodus 25:20. These angels were to look down upon the ark, showing the respect which Heaven has for God's law. God further said, "There I will meet with thee, and I will commune with thee from above the mercy seat, from between the two cherubims." Verse 22. Above the ark was the throne of the Infinite, and inside the ark was the law of love containing the principles of the divine government. David prayed, "Thou that dwellest between the cherubims, shine forth." Psalm 80:1. God dwelt mystically "between the cherubims" in the earthly sanctuary; and there mercy had its "seat," or source, and from there pardon was granted for the violation of the law of love in the ark.

All this constituted "figures" of the true sanctuary in heaven, and today "Christ is not entered into the holy places made with hands, which are the figures of the true; but into heaven itself, now to appear in the presence of God for us." Hebrews 9:24. There Jesus, as our High Priest, mediates for sinners. But what is sin? We have the answer in 1 John 3:4: "Sin is the transgression of the law." Which law? We find the answer in Revelation 11:19: "The temple of God was opened in heaven, and there was seen in his temple the ark of his testament." There we find the real ark; there we find the real Priest; there we find the real mediation; and there we find in "the ark of his testament"—the real Ten Commandments after which the earthly was patterned. If the law that was in the ark was abrogated at the cross, Christ is mediating for the transgression of an abrogated law!

These are irrefutable truths which escape the mind of the man who holds this sacred law in contempt. The very fact that the original of this law is in heaven, where Christ, our High Priest, mediates His blood for pardon, shows how impossible it is for this law to be cast down. No stronger argument could be produced to prove that the Decalogue is not abolished. And today, just as certainly as in the earthly ark, it reads, "The seventh day is the sabbath," else it would not be a true pattern.

In the Old Testament sin is defined as doing "somewhat against any of the commandments of the Lord concerning things which ought not to be done" (Leviticus 4:27); and in the New Testament it is the same: "Sin is the transgression of the law" (1 John 3:4). In the Old Testament these commandments of the Lord were kept in the ark, in the holy of holies, where God dwelt. This ark was called "the ark of the testimony." Years after the cross John was permitted to see the temple above, and he says there was seen in God's temple "the ark of his testament." So there it is today, defining sin; and there Jesus is, too, mediating His blood for the transgression of the law.

Legalism No New Issue

It will be of interest to inquire, How did this matter of what was abolished and what was not abolished happen to come up in some of the apostolic discussions? The answer, as we hope to prove, is plain. Some came along, after the apostles had raised up churches and gone on to other places, and taught the new converts that they should go back to the practicing of circumcision and the keeping of new moons and festivals.

We get an instance of this in Acts 15:1: "And certain men which came down from Judaea taught the brethren, and said, Except ye be circumcised after the manner of Moses, ye cannot be saved." In verse five we have this injunction repeated: "But there rose up certain of the sect of the Pharisees which believed, saying, That it was needful to circumcise them, and to command them to keep the law of Moses." This text does not refer to the law of the Ten Commandments, for there is nothing in it about circumcision. Paul puts a distinction between the two laws when he declares in 1 Corinthians 7:19: "Circumcision is nothing, and uncircumcision is nothing; but the keeping of the commandments of God." It is unscriptural to claim that Acts 15:1, 5 discusses whether Christians should keep the Ten Commandments.

The same matter came up in the church at Galatia. Paul said: "And that because of false brethren unawares brought in, who came in privily to spy out our liberty which we have in Christ Jesus, that they might bring us into bondage." Galatians 2:4. What was this bondage? Was it (as antinomians teach) that Paul's gospel had given them "liberty . . . in Christ Jesus" to worship idols, profane the Lord's name and the Sabbath day, murder, lie, steal, commit adultery? Is that what Paul meant?

How is it possible for those who claim to be Christians and ministers of God to hold such a view? We again inquire, What was this bondage? Let us turn to Galatians 5:1, 2 and read what it was: "Stand fast therefore in the liberty wherewith Christ hath made us free, and be not entangled again with the yoke of bondage. Behold, I Paul say unto you, that if ye be circumcised, Christ shall profit you nothing." Is there anything in the Ten Commandments about circumcision? Obviously it was not the Ten Commandment law of which Paul was speaking.

This fact is explained further in Galatians 4:9, 10: "How turn ye again to the weak and beggarly elements, whereunto ye desire again to be in bondage? Ye observe days, and months, and times, and years." Is there anything in the Ten Commandments about days (plural), months, times, and years? Not one word. They were all found in the other law which Moses gave to the people.

These discussions did not come up because the apostles taught Christians to practice the immoralities condemned by the Ten Commandments and then false teachers came along and attempted to stop the practice of such sins. It was because these false teachers attempted to get Christians back to the observances of "the law of commandments contained in ordinances" which were abolished at the cross (Ephesians 2:15). Many of these pointed ahead to the death of Christ, and to practice them after the cross was a denial that He had died.

Here are some verses in Hebrews that are often misapplied to the Ten Commandments:

"For the priesthood being changed, there is made of necessity a change also of the law. For he [Christ] of whom these things are spoken pertaineth to another tribe, of which no man gave attendance at the altar. For it is evident that our Lord sprang out of [the tribe of] Juda; of which tribe Moses spake nothing concerning priesthood." Hebrews 7:12–14.

Paul is not speaking of the law of Ten Commandments, but of the law of the priesthood. According to this law, no one but a Levite could be a priest (Numbers 3:9, 10). But after the death of Jesus the priesthood was changed. It was changed from earth to heaven (Hebrews 8:1–3), and from the tribe of Levi to the tribe of Judah. Therefore, the law that regulated the priesthood had to be changed in order that Christ, who sprang from the tribe of Judah, could be made priest. Just why men will read these verses and declare they have reference to the Ten Commandments is hard to understand. What is more tragic? An ordinary audience knows so little about the Scriptures that they will accept this wresting of the Scriptures, thinking it to be the truth.

Chapter 9

The Two Covenants

For the sake of truth, and as a safeguard against deception, let us consider at this time the claim that the Ten Commandment law is the old covenant. Those who make this claim do so in an attempt to prove that the observance of the seventh day passed away with the old covenant and is, therefore, no longer obligatory. Of course if this is true of the seventh day, it is also true of those duties enjoined by the other nine commandments as well; and that which proves too much proves nothing. Many scriptures are used, or rather misused, to prove this claim, all of which is confusing to those who do not clearly understand the Bible truth concerning the two covenants.

It is well first to state the arguments of those who use the question of the covenants to oppose the observance of the seventh day in order to see whether they are "rightly dividing the word of truth." Then we will take up three propositions: (1) What the old covenant was not. (2) What the old covenant was. (3) What the new covenant is.

The proponents of the claim that the Decalogue is the old covenant read Hebrews 8:13, which says, "In that he saith, A new covenant, he hath made the first old. Now that which decayeth and waxeth old is ready to vanish away." They emphasize the fact that the old covenant has vanished away, and Christians are under the new covenant, to which claim Sabbathkeepers certainly agree. But it does not follow that this old covenant is the law of the Ten Commandments.

The no-law preachers next go to Galatians 4:24 to prove that the old covenant originated at Mount Sinai and hence (according to their understanding) must be the Ten Commandments. Galatians 4:24 reads: "For these are the two covenants; the one [old covenant] from the mount Sinai, which gendereth to bondage." Paul is comparing the bondage of the old covenant with the liberty of the new by contrasting Hagar and Ishmael (who were bondslaves of Abraham) with Sarah and Isaac (who were free). (Verses 22–31). It is true that Paul plainly says that this old covenant which gendered to bondage and passed away was "from the mount Sinai." And it is true that the Ten Commandments were given from Mount Sinai.

It is also true that the Ten Commandments are called a "covenant" in Deuteronomy 4:13, which reads: "He declared unto you his covenant, which he commanded you to perform, even ten commandments; and he wrote them upon two tables of stone." They are also called a "covenant" in Deuteronomy 9:9–11: "When I was gone up into the mount to receive the tables of stone, even the tables of the covenant which the Lord made with you, then I abode in the mount forty days and forty nights. . . . The Lord gave me the two tables of stone, even the tables of the covenant." With no more careful attention to all that occurred at Sinai, these texts would seem to prove the Ten Commandments to be the old covenant that passed away. If this contention is true, then of course the observance of the Sabbath passed away too, since it is one of the Ten Commandments.

Some No-Law Arguments Examined

There are two more verses which can be added to the citations already made in the attempt to prove the Ten Commandments to be the old covenant. These two verses, 1 Kings 8:21 and 9, seemingly clinch the argument. These verses read: "I have set there a place for the ark, wherein is the covenant of the Lord, which he made with our fathers, when he brought them out of the land of Egypt." "There was nothing in the ark save the two tables of stone, which Moses put there at Horeb." Notice that in this ark there was a complete "covenant."

All the verses cited (and especially the last two) do prove beyond all question that the law of Ten Commandments does constitute *one of the covenants* which the Lord made with Israel at Sinai. God made two covenants with the Israelites at Mount Sinai—one in the nineteenth chapter of Exodus and, three days later, another in the twentieth chapter of Exodus, where the Ten Commandments covenant is found. Thus the Decalogue is not the *old* covenant which waxed old and vanished away. This assertion will be better understood when it is shown from the Scriptures how impossible it is to apply Paul's descriptions of the old covenant to the Ten Commandments.

Speaking of the defects of the old covenant, Paul declares in Hebrews 8:6: "But now hath he [Christ] obtained a more excellent ministry, by how much also he is the mediator of a better covenant, which was established upon better promises." Here we have the evidence that something was wrong with some of the promises of the old covenant, and that the new covenant is established upon better ones. Examine the Ten Commandments one by one to discover in them the poor promises. As yet no one has ever found anything weak or wrong with the promises found in the Ten Commandments.

In Ephesians 6:1–3, on this very point, Paul says, "Children, obey your parents in the Lord: for this is right. Honour thy father and mother; which is the first commandment with promise; that it may be well with thee, and thou mayest live long on the earth." This is the fifth commandment, and it is the first of the ten with a promise: that of long life to children who obey their parents.

Can anyone find anything wrong with this promise? Paul is here quoting directly from the Ten Commandments, not from some portion of the New Testament writings, and this proves that Paul still believed in these commandments and their observance. He did not believe they had been abolished. Then if in Paul's day the fifth commandment of the ten was still binding, the fourth, which declares, "The seventh day is the sabbath of the Lord," was still binding. It is scripturally impossible for the Ten Commandments to be the old covenant, for there are no defective promises found therein.

Continuing the study of what the old covenant is not, I turn to another defect in the old covenant, mentioned in Hebrews 8:7 as follows; "For if that first covenant had been faultless, then should no place have been sought for the second." Here we find that it was on account of the faults (in addition to the poor promises) of this old covenant that it was done away with. But no amount of examination of the Ten Commandments has ever discovered any faults in them. Yet if the Ten Commandments constitute the old covenant, then the faults must be there. No one, however, would presume even to attempt to prove that a law which the Lord Himself proclaimed with His own voice was here and there defective and faulty.

When the Lord commanded that man refrain from idolatry, from desecrating His name and His day, from dishonoring parents, from murder, theft, adultery, lying, and coveting, did He later discover that such commands were faulty because they imposed a burdensome yoke upon the carnal nature, and should therefore vanish away and set man at liberty? This is the logical conclusion of the claim that the Ten Commandments are the old covenant.

That the Ten Commandments have no faults in them is clearly proven by the Scriptures. In Psalm 19:7 we are told: "The law of the Lord is perfect, converting the soul." Paul declares, "Wherefore the law is holy, and the commandment holy, and just, and good." Romans 7:12. How could anything be holy and just and good and faulty at the same time? Surely this proves that the descriptions of the old covenant do not fit the Ten Commandments. But when we come to what really is the old covenant, we find promises that were not good, we find faults, and we discover why it gendered to bondage and vanished away.

Speaking again of the old covenant, Paul said: "In that he saith, A new covenant, he hath made the first old. Now that which decayeth and waxeth old is ready to vanish away." Hebrews 8:13. This certainly proves that time and necessity made void the old covenant, and it passed away. But what about the law? Had it been made void, too, in Paul's day? If the law and the old covenant are one and the same thing, it certainly had become void. But what says the apostle Paul concerning the law? In Romans 3:31 he states, "Do we then make void the law through faith? God forbid: yea, we establish the law." How could something be established in the letter to the Romans and the same thing be abolished and done away with in the epistle to the Hebrews? Suppose we put "old covenant" in Romans 3:31 instead of "law" and see how it reads: "Do we then make void the old covenant through faith? God forbid: yea, we establish the old covenant." That changed reading would be scripturally correct if it be true that the law and the old covenant are one and the same. But the absurdity of the change certainly puts to shame the argument which contends that the law is the old covenant.

Just What Was the Old Covenant?

Having found that the old covenant is not the Ten Commandments, we are now ready to go to the nineteenth chapter of Exodus and there find what the old covenant is. Before we do so, however, let us note that we have certainly found that the Ten Commandments are said to be a covenant which the Lord made with the house of Israel at Mount Sinai. This covenant is found in the twentieth chapter of Exodus. Now, I repeat, if we find another covenant made three days before in the nineteenth chapter of Exodus, that will be two covenants made at Sinai. That more than one covenant was made with Israel is proved by Paul's language in Romans 9:4: "Who are Israelites; to whom pertaineth the adoption, and the glory, and the covenants, and the giving of the law, and the service of God, and the promises." Here we have the proof of "covenants" (plural) made with the Israelites. Now let us consider the old covenant.

That the covenant of the nineteenth chapter of Exodus was made at Mount Sinai is proven by reading the first two verses of this chapter: "In the third month, when the children of Israel were gone forth out of the land of Egypt, the same day came they into the wilderness of Sinai. . . . And there Israel camped before the mount." Here we have the Israelites at the foot of Mount Sinai.

Now comes the preamble of the old covenant: "And Moses went up unto God, and the Lord called unto him out of the mountain, saying, Thus shalt thou say to the house of Jacob, and tell the children of Israel; Ye have seen what I did unto the Egyptians, and how I bare you on eagles' wings, and brought you unto myself." Exodus 19:3, 4.

Next comes God's part of the contract, or covenant: "Now therefore, if ye will obey my voice indeed, and keep my covenant, then ye shall be a peculiar treasure unto me above all people: for all the earth is mine: and ye shall be unto me a kingdom of priests, and an holy nation. These are the words which thou shalt speak unto the children of Israel." Exodus 19:5, 6.

If we find that the Israelites accepted this proposition, we shall have discovered a covenant, plain and simple, between the Lord and them at Mount Sinai, recorded in the nineteenth chapter of Exodus, and made three days before the Ten Commandment covenant of Exodus 20. Did the Israelites enter into this covenant with God after Moses put the proposition to them? We read that they did, and now comes the peoples' part of the covenant: "And Moses came and called for the elders of the people, and laid before their faces all these words which the Lord commanded him. And all the people answered together, and said, All that the Lord hath spoken we will do. And Moses returned the words of the people unto the Lord." Exodus 19:7, 8. This old covenant, in which the people did the promising, was repeated twice again (Exodus 24:3–8), and it was ratified with the blood of animal sacrifices.

This is the old covenant spoken of by Paul in the eighth chapter of Hebrews which proved faulty, had poor promises, gendered to bondage, and vanished away because, as we shall see, the people never kept those promises. They failed to live up to their part of the covenant, thereby forfeiting the promises God had made unto them.

Nature of the New Covenant

This makes way for the third question: What is the new covenant? I turn first to Jeremiah 31:31–33.

"Behold, the days come, saith the Lord, that I will make a new covenant with the house of Israel, and with the house of Judah: not according to the covenant that I made with their fathers in the day that I took them by the hand to bring them out of the land of Egypt; which my covenant they brake, although I was an husband unto them, saith the Lord: but this shall be the covenant that I will make with the house of Israel; After those days, saith the Lord, I will put my law in their inward parts, and write it in their hearts; and will be their God, and they shall be my people."

The new covenant is: "I will put my law [then in existence] in their inward parts, and write it in their hearts." Here are the "better promises" of the new covenant, better because God makes them. God's "I will" is sure, but the people's "we will" proved to be faulty and gendered to bondage.

We are now ready for Hebrews 8:6–10, where the two covenants, the old and the new, are contrasted.

"But now hath he obtained a more excellent ministry, by how much also he is the mediator of a better covenant, which was established upon better promises. For if that first covenant [made in Exodus 19 and 24, when Moses acted as the mediator] had been faultless, then should no place have been sought for the second. For finding fault with them [the people, for breaking their promises of the Exodus 19 covenant], he saith, Behold, the days come, saith the Lord, when I will make a new covenant with the house of Israel and with the house of Judah: not according to the covenant that I made with their fathers in the day when I took them by the hand to lead them out of the land of Egypt; because they continued not in my covenant, and I regarded them not, saith the Lord. For this is the covenant that I will make with the house of Israel after those days, saith the Lord; I will put my laws into their mind, and write them in their hearts: and I will be to them a God, and they shall be to me a people."

All these promises are divine. They are made by One who is able to carry them out. It is thus that the new covenant is established upon better promises.

What Made the Difference?

The fundamental difference between the old covenant and the new is that in ancient times the people understood the performance of spiritual duties through human effort, saying, "We will do." This could not be done then, nor can it be done now. "For," says Paul, "we know that the law is spiritual." Romans 7:14. This explains why "the carnal mind . . . is not subject to the law of God, neither indeed can be." Romans 8:7. The new-covenant people are made spiritual by the regenerative operation of the Holy Spirit on their hearts, then the law which is spiritual is written on their hearts, and thus obedience becomes divinely performed through the indwelling Christ. "For what the law could not do, in that it was weak through the flesh, God sending his own Son in the likeness of sinful flesh, and for sin, condemned [conquered] sin in the flesh: that the righteousness of the law might be fulfilled in us." Romans 8:3, 4. Note that the requirements of the law are not fulfilled *by* us but *in* us.

Speaking of this new, or everlasting, covenant and its advantages, Paul says: "Now the God of peace, that brought again from the dead our Lord Jesus, that great shepherd of the sheep, through the blood of the everlasting covenant, make you perfect in every good work to do his will, working in you that which is well pleasing in his sight, through Jesus Christ." Hebrews 13:20, 21. The old covenant (Exodus 19) proposition of "we will do" ended in failure; but the proposition of God "working in you . . . through Jesus Christ" means victory. There is no other way that the requirements of a spiritual law can be lived out in the flesh.

In the face of these scriptural evidences, what becomes of the human arguments claiming God's law was abolished at the cross? Would God write the principles of an abrogated law in the hearts of His people? Would God include obedience to an abolished law in the new covenant? The working of the new covenant proves that the new-covenant people cannot be those who are in rebellion against the Ten Commandments. Remember, too, that this law written in the hearts of God's people includes the commandment which declares, "The seventh day is the sabbath of the Lord."

This new covenant, or new statement, does not include the observance of the first day of the week, Sunday, as a new-covenant duty; for, according to the advocates of first-day observance, the first day did not originate as a duty until after the death of Christ. Everyone knows that after the death of a man nothing can be added or taken from his will and testament. The death of the testator ratifies the will, or testament. Then if the observance of the first day of the week is a New Testament duty, it had to be put into the new covenant before the death of Christ; and since it was not, that scripturally excludes it.

The Lord's Supper and the New Covenant

Now we are ready for some Bible texts on this point. In Hebrews 9:16, 17 we read: "For where a testament is, there must also of necessity be the death of the testator. For a testament is of force after men are dead: otherwise it is of no strength at all while the testator liveth."

This explains why Jesus, before His death, instituted the Lord's Supper. It would be too late to get it into the new covenant after He died. So we read: "And as they were eating, Jesus took bread, and blessed it, and brake it, and gave it to the disciples, and said, Take, eat; this is my body. And he took the cup, and gave thanks, and gave it to them, saying, Drink ye all of it; for this is my blood of the new testament [or covenant], which is shed for many for the remission of sins." Matthew 26:26–28.

So in order to get the Lord's Supper into the new covenant, it was necessary that it be put there before the death of the Testator. "For," says Paul, "a testament is of force after men are dead." Then how could the observance of the first day of the week originate as a new-covenant duty after the death of Christ, the Testator? That such a thing was impossible is stated by Paul in Galatians 3:15, where he declares, "Though it be but a man's covenant, yet if it be confirmed [by death], no man disannulleth, or addeth thereto." If Jesus Himself could not add to the Lord's Supper after His death, how could Constantine, the papal church, the disciples, or anyone else add the observance of the first day of the week as a new-covenant duty after the death of Christ? His death ratified, confirmed, finished, and closed up the new covenant, which, says Paul, was of force after the death of the Testator, Christ.

A certain opponent of the true Sabbath once wrote that, after the death of our Lord, the leaders of the early church set apart the first day of the week as the day to be kept. A logical mind can only conclude that until these leaders did this, the seventh day must have continued to be observed. Or was there an interval between the "abolition" of the seventh day and the later setting apart of the first day? I wonder how such an argument, of "the setting apart by the leaders of the early church of Sunday as a day of worship," can be propounded in the face of the *fact* that Jesus, the Testator of the new covenant, ratified it by His death on the cross.

New Covenant Christians

In conclusion we have found (1) that the old covenant is not the Ten Commandments, (2) that the old covenant is the agreement between God and Israel found in the first part of the nineteenth chapter of Exodus, and (3) that the new covenant is summed up in Hebrews 8:10: "I will put my laws into their mind, and write them in their hearts: and I will be to them a God, and they shall be to me a people."

It seems that since there is a new covenant people, they could be discovered by the fact that they will have the commandments written in their hearts. The Bible says, "Out of it [the heart] are the issues of life." This makes it plain that those who have the commandments in the heart will be constant, living witnesses for them. On the other hand those who are not new covenant Christians will be constantly preaching against the Ten Commandments because they are not in their hearts. God cannot write in the heart that which the heart rebels against.

We have seen that the principle of the old covenant was that of righteousness by the works of the law, which then and now leads to bondage; and that the principle of the new covenant is that of righteousness by faith, which leads to freedom.

Light From an Allegory

The truth that the old covenant is based on the principle of what man attempts to do alone and fails—as contrasted with the new covenant, which is based on what God does with man—is supported and proven by Paul's illustration of the two wives of Abraham: Hagar, the wife of bondage, with her son Ishmael; and Sarah, the wife of freedom, and her son Isaac. When we understand this illustration, we shall see how far they who contend that the old covenant is the law of Ten Commandments miss the mark. Please read carefully the following:

"Tell me, ye that desire to be under the law, do ye not hear the law? For it is written, that Abraham had two sons, the one by a bondmaid, the other by a freewoman. But he who was of the bondwoman was born after the flesh; but he of the freewoman was by promise. Which things are an allegory: for these are the two covenants; the one from the mount Sinai, which gendereth to bondage, which is Agar. For this Agar is mount Sinai in Arabia, and answereth to Jerusalem which now is, and is in bondage with her children. But Jerusalem which is above is free, which is the mother of us all. For it is written, Rejoice, thou barren that bearest not;

break forth and cry, thou that travailest not: for the desolate hath many more children than she which hath an husband. Now we, brethren, as Isaac was, are the children of promise. But as then he that was born after the flesh persecuteth him that was born after the Spirit, even so it is now. Nevertheless what saith the scripture? Cast out the bondwoman and her son: for the son of the bondwoman shall not be heir with the son of the freewoman. So then, brethren, we are not children of the bondwoman, but of the free." Galatians 4:21–31.

Then Paul continues:

"Stand fast therefore in the liberty wherewith Christ hath made us free, and be not entangled again with the yoke of bondage. Behold, I Paul say unto you, that if ye be circumcised, Christ shall profit you nothing. For I testify again to every man that is circumcised, that he is debtor to do the whole law. Christ is become of no effect unto you, whosoever of you are justified by the law; ye are fallen from grace. For we through the Spirit wait for the hope of righteousness by faith."

These last verses are quoted from Galatians 5:1–5 and are a continuation of the points Paul was trying to make in the illustration of the bondwoman and her son, representing the old covenant from Sinai, and the freewoman and her son, representing the subjects of the new covenant.

Before studying further into the meaning of all this, we should first look into the interpretation of this allegory by the dispensationalists and other no-law teachers. In the first place, this allegory is directed to "ye that desire to be under the law" (Galatians 4:21). It is claimed that Paul here has reference to the Ten Commandments and is against those who respect them. If we put that interpretation into this text, it would have to read, "Tell men, ye that desire to refrain from idolatry, stealing, lying, murder, profanity, Sabbath desecration, etc., do ye not hear the law? But here the words "the law" have reference to something written in Genesis.

This is proven by the fact that after he asks, "Do ye not hear the law?" he immediately follows this by saying, "For it is written." Written where? Written in the law that said, "Abraham had two sons." This positively proves Paul was not quoting from the Ten Commandments but from the book of Genesis, which he called "the law." Incidentally Jesus called Psalm 82:6 "your law" (John 10:34).

Let us suppose that after Paul had said, "Tell me, ye that desire to be under the law, do ye not hear the law?" he had gone on as follows: "for it is written, Thou shalt have no other gods before me. Thou shalt not make unto thee any graven image. Thou shalt not take the name of the Lord thy God in vain. Remember the Sabbath day, to keep it holy." If that is what had followed after Paul said, "For it is written," it would suit the opponents of this law a great deal better than the things which Paul did say after saying, "It is written." But notwithstanding the fact that he started quoting from Genesis rather than from the twentieth chapter of Exodus, the dispensationalists still must have it that when Paul said "the law" here, he had his mind exclusively on the Ten Commandments.

Going back to Abraham and Sarah, we find that after the failure—based on "we will"—to produce a son, God said, "Sarah thy wife shall bear thee a son indeed; and thou shalt call his name Isaac." Genesis 17:19. At that time Sarah was not only barren, but "she was past age" (Hebrews 11:11). But "the Lord visited Sarah," and "Sarah conceived, and bare Abraham a son in his old age." Genesis 21:1, 2.

It required a supernatural act of God to bring this son into being. Paul calls him the child of promise. He was not "born after the flesh," but "after the Spirit" (Galatians 4:29). Just so, on account of the fact that "the flesh is weak," man cannot attain to the righteousness of the law. For if this is to be done, there must be a supernatural working of the power of God, as in the case of Isaac. All attempts on the old-covenant basis of "we will do" will produce only children of bondage. But when the heart is yielded to God, when the Holy Spirit writes the principles of the law in the "tables of the heart," we become "the children . . . of the free." When these principles of love as expressed in "the letter" on "tables of stone" are transferred to the "tables of the heart" by the working of God's power through the Holy Spirit, then "the righteousness of the law" is fulfilled in us" (Romans 8:1–4), or, in other words, Isaac is born.

So instead of Paul's illustration teaching that the commandments are abolished, it teaches that through the operation of the Holy Spirit provision is made for obedience. Ishmael represents those who are "born after the flesh" and are "not subject to the law of God, neither indeed can be" (Romans 8:7). Isaac represents those who are "born after the Spirit," in whom "the righteousness of the law" is being fulfilled. Thus do we clearly see that the commandment-breakers are the children of bondage, and the commandment-keepers (through Christ) are the children of the free.

Jesus made this plain in John 8:34, 35: "Jesus answered them, Verily, verily I say unto you, whosoever committeth sin is the servant of sin.

And the servant abideth not in the house forever." This last statement about the servant not abiding in the house reminds me of the words, "Cast out the bondwoman and her son." Then Jesus continued, "If the Son therefore shall make you free, ye shall be free indeed." Observe carefully. Who is the servant of sin? The answer is, "Whosoever committeth sin." Again we inquire, What is sin? The answer to that question is, "Sin is the transgression of the law." 1 John 3:4. Then who are the Ishmaelites of the old covenant? The answer is evident. They are those who live in transgression of God's holy law.

In Paul's allegory Ishmael, who was "born after the flesh," persecuted Isaac, who was "born after the Spirit." Revelation 12:17 says, "The dragon was wroth with the woman [church], and went to make war with the remnant of her seed, which keep the commandments of God, and have the testimony of Jesus Christ." There is no such thing as persecution against Sunday-keeping, but many are the records in our own free America of the observers of the seventh day having been thrown into prison. In almost every instance this has been done at the instigation of religious leaders who preach that the Ten Commandments are abolished.

We are now ready to sum up Paul's illustration of the contrast between the principles of the old and new covenants.

God promised Abraham a son. After long waiting, he received no son. "Sarai Abram's wife bare him no children." Then instead of waiting longer and trusting God to solve the problem, "Sarai said unto Abram, Behold now, the Lord hath restrained me from bearing: I pray thee, go in unto my maid; it may be that I may obtain children by her. And Abram hearkened to the voice of Sarai. And Hagar bare Abram a son: and Abram called the son's name, which Hagar bare, Ishmael. And Abram was fourscore and six years old, when Hagar bare Ishmael to Abram." Genesis 16:1, 2, 15. Paul says this son was "born after the flesh" and was in "bondage" because his mother was a slave in Abraham's household. Instead of Abraham's recognizing that because of Sarah's barenness and age there was nothing he could do to produce a son, and that God would have to do this for him by the operation of divine power, he hearkened unto Sarah and undertook the impossible on the basis of "we will do" through Hagar. The result was a child of bondage whom God cast out and could not accept.

Here we have the principle of the old covenant. When God in Exodus 19:5–8 said to Israel, "If ye will obey my voice indeed, and keep my covenant, then ye shall be a peculiar treasure unto me above all people," instead of saying, "We will do," they should have said, "Lord, we of ourselves can do nothing. We pray you to work out that obedience in us." But instead of this, just as Abraham did, they set out to do by their own works that which only God could do, and the result was bondage and slavery to condemnation. This transaction between God and Israel was at Mount Sinai, where Israel camped before the mount (Exodus 19:2). This is why Paul in speaking of that covenant said, "The one from the mount Sinai . . . gendereth to bondage." Galatians 4:24.

Chapter 10

"The Ministration of Death"

To introduce this subject, I offer the following parenthetical treatment of 2 Corinthians 3:7–16:

"But if the ministration of death [for the violation of the commandments], written and engraven in stones, was glorious ["came with glory," A.S.V.], so that the children of Israel could not stedfastly behold the face of Moses for the glory of his countenance; which glory [ministration] was to be done away: how shall not the ministration of the spirit be rather glorious? For if the ministration of condemnation be glory, much more doth the ministration of righteousness exceed in glory. For even that which was made glorious had no glory in this respect, by reason of the glory that excelleth. For if that [ministration] which is done away was glorious, much more that [ministration] which remaineth is glorious. Seeing then that we have such hope, we use great plainness of speech: and not as Moses, which put a vail over his face, that the children of Israel could not stedfastly look to the end of that [ministration] which is abolished: but their minds were blinded: for until this day remaineth the same vail [which was illustrated by the vail on Moses' face] untaken away in the reading of the old testament [Scriptures which testify of Christ]; which vail [blindness] is done away in Christ. . . . Nevertheless when it [that blinded heart] shall turn to the Lord, the vail shall be taken away."

Let us carefully note that Paul is not discussing the law, but "the ministration" of the law. The word "ministration" is translated "administration" in 1 Corinthians 12:5. Back in the days of Moses the "administration" pronounced immediate death for presumptuous violations of the commandments. In Paul's day and under his ministry such was not the case. Please note that the difference lay not with the law but with the "ministrations." Paul contrasts "the ministrations of death" and "the ministration of the Spirit." The "ministration of condemnation" was followed by "the ministration of righteousness." There is all the difference in the world between the law itself and the administration of the law. When the administration of the Constitution changes from the Democratic Party to the Republican, the Constitution is not changed. It is left intact. So with the law of Ten Commandments.

The following texts clearly show what Paul meant by the term "ministration of death"; they also show that the law he referred to was the Decalogue.

"And he that blasphemeth the name of the Lord, he shall surely be put to death." Leviticus 24:16. "Whosoever doeth any work in the sabbath day, he shall surely be put to death." Exodus 31:15. "For every one that curseth his father or his mother shall be surely put to death." Leviticus 20:9. "And he that killeth any man shall surely be put to death." Leviticus 24:17. "The adulterer and the adulteress shall surely be put to death." Leviticus 20:10.

It should be kept in mind that in Moses' day Israel was called a "nation" and also "the church in the wilderness" (Numbers 14:12; Acts 7:38). The church and the nation were united under the immediate direction of God; it was a union of church and state. Such a regime is a theocracy. But the time came when the Israelites demanded a king to judge them "like all the nations." In granting this request, the Lord said, "They have rejected me, that I should not reign over them." 1 Samuel 8:7. It was then that "the ministration of death" for civil offenses passed into the hands of kings and civil courts, and the theocracy was abolished, or "done away," as we read in 2 Corinthians 3.

When Jesus came to earth and was tried by the Jewish leaders, they said, "We have a law, and by our law he ought to die." John 19:7. He was charged with blasphemy: "Now ye have heard his blasphemy, What think ye? They answered and said, He is guilty of death." Matthew 26:65, 66. But the power to put Him to death had passed out of their hands, and they appealed to the Roman government for permission to kill the Saviour. Thus "the ministration of death," which, in Moses's day, was invested in the church, had been abolished. Of course Jesus Himself taught the doctrine of the separation of church and state, for He said, "Render therefore unto Caesar the things which are Caesar's; and unto God the things that are God's." Matthew 22:20, 21.

Under the theocracy it was declared, "The judgment is God's: and the cause that is too hard for you, bring it unto me and I will hear it." Deuteronomy 1:17. It was God working through Moses who pronounced the conviction and the sentence. Moses was a minister of God in both civil and spiritual matters. The authority of both church and state resided in him.

Paul served as God's minister under a "more glorious" administration, "the ministration of the spirit" (2 Corinthians 3:8). Instead of executing "the ministration of death" upon the guilty, Paul preached the gospel unto them under the power of the Holy Spirit. This was "the ministration of the spirit."

We have an illustration of this ministration in 1 Corinthians 6:9–11: "Know ye not that the unrighteous shall not inherit the kingdom of God? Be not deceived: neither fornicators, nor idolaters, nor adulterers, . . . nor thieves, . . . shall inherit the kingdom of God. And such were some of you: but ye are washed, but ye are sanctified, but ye are justified, in the name of the Lord Jesus, and by the Spirit of our God."

There are some more important truths about theocracy which should be understood before leaving the subject. It was only the sins that were committed daringly and "with an high hand" (Numbers 15:30, margin) that called forth the ministration of death. For other sins an offering was brought, and they were forgiven. Thus we read: "And if any should sin through ignorance, then he shall bring a she goat of the first year for a sin offering. And the priest shall make an atonement for the soul that sinneth ignorantly, . . . and it shall be forgiven him. But the soul that doeth ought presumptuously, . . . the same reproacheth the Lord [he hath despised the word of the Lord]; . . . and that soul shall be cut off from among his people." Numbers 15:27–31. It was God who decided concerning the nature of the sin. But Paul was not living under that regime, for it had been abolished.

The argument is often made, and with some show of triumph, that since the death penalty for the violation of the law is no longer executed by the Lord, the law too is gone, and that for a law to be valid there must be the penalty for its violation.

May I remind such that the death penalty has been deferred to the day of judgment. He has reserved "the unjust unto the day of judgment to be punished" (2 Peter 2:9). "Sin is the transgression of the law" (1 John 3:4), and "the wages of sin is death" (Romans 6:23), and "sin, when it is finished, bringeth forth death." James 1:15. Punishment for civil offenses has been transferred to the civil powers (Romans 13:1). But in the sense that the same transgressions are a sin against God, the guilty one, if he does not repent, will be eternally lost.

Chapter 11

Concluding Facts

Perhaps there is no claim heard more frequently than this: "It makes no difference which day you keep holy, just so you keep a day." But the question is, Can one keep a day holy that the Lord has never made holy? Can man take the holiness and sanctification of one day and place it upon another? Suppose someone should hand you a soiled garment and tell you to keep it clean. How could you keep it clean when it is not clean to start with? Then how can a person keep a day holy that is not holy to start with?

The fourth commandment says, "Remember the sabbath day, to keep it holy." We know that the word "Sabbath" means "rest." Then we are commanded to keep the rest day holy. Of whose rest day is the Bible speaking? We read: "For in six days the Lord made heaven and earth, the sea, and all that in them is, and rested the seventh day: wherefore the Lord blessed the sabbath day, and hallowed it." Exodus 20:11.

This text makes it plain that the Lord blessed the day on which He rested. That act made it the Sabbath day—the "rest" day. There were six days on which He did not rest. None of these could be His rest day. He blessed and made holy the day on which He rested, and no other. Then a man is not keeping the Creator's rest day if the seventh part of time he observes falls on one of the days on which the Lord worked. The first, second, third, fourth, fifth, and sixth days of the week are called in God's Word "the six working days" (Ezekiel 46:1). They are the days on which the Creator worked. He did not rest on one of these days, nor did He bless any of them. The commandment says that the Creator blessed the day on which He rested, and then it tells us that this was the seventh day.

Miracles Confirm the Sabbath

The falling of the manna for forty years in the wilderness certainly emphasized that the Sabbath was one particular day. No other day could be substituted. The Lord told Israel that He was going to rain bread from heaven for them in order to prove whether they would walk in His law or not (Exodus 16:4). They were to gather just the amount they needed each day, and if they gathered more than that and laid it up until the next day, it spoiled and was unfit to eat. So on the "sixth day they gathered twice as much bread." Moses told them:

"This is that which the Lord hath said, Tomorrow is the rest of the holy sabbath unto the Lord: . . . that which remaineth over lay up for you to be kept until the morning. And they laid it up till the morning, as Moses bade: and it did not stink, neither was there any worm therein. And Moses said, Eat that to day; for to day is a sabbath unto the Lord: to day ye shall not find it in the field. Six days ye shall gather it; but on the seventh day, which is the sabbath, in it there shall be none. And it came to pass, that there went out some of the people on the seventh day for to gather, and they found none. And the Lord said unto Moses, How long refuse ye to keep my commandments and my laws?" Exodus 16:23–28.

We gather from this narrative the following Bible facts concerning the forty years of manna:

1. It was to be a test of obedience.
2. The manna fell only six days in the week.
3. If they gathered more than they needed, it spoiled.
4. On the sixth day they were to gather a double portion.
5. They were to lay up some of this for the Sabbath.
6. God worked a miracle to keep it fresh over the Sabbath.
7. When they went out on the seventh day to gather, they found none.
8. God called this act a violation of His law.

Let us suppose we lived in those days and contended, as some of the Israelites did, that the Sabbath was not a particular day, but that it could be any day. Suppose we contended that we were going to let our seventh part of time fall on the second day of the week. We went out on the first day and gathered a double portion of food. But the next morning when we went to eat our breakfast, we found it spoiled and full of worms.

So we see the "not-any-day-in-particular" and "just-any-day" theories do not work. The Lord does not countenance any such juggling of His Word.

The New Testament makes it equally plain that the Sabbath is a particular day. After placing the body of Jesus in Joseph's new sepulcher on "the day before the sabbath" (Mark 15:42), Jesus' followers "returned, and prepared spices and ointments, and rested the sabbath day according to the commandment." Luke 23:56. There can be but one day that is "the sabbath day according to the commandment," because it is the day on which the Lord rested, and He rested on the seventh day, and no other. Then the New Testament makes it plain that "the sabbath day according to the commandment" is a definite day—the day following the crucifixion.

The Sabbath on a Round World

But how can the Sabbath be kept on a round world with its many time zones? This question was answered when Jesus declared, "The sabbath was made for man" (Mark 2:27), and when Paul declared that God made "all nations of men for to dwell on all the face of the earth" (Acts 17:26). This shows that wherever man dwells, the Sabbath was made for him. His location on the globe does not rob him of the Sabbath blessing. So in reality the argument on this matter is with God's Word and not with those who still observe the Sabbath day. Sabbathkeepers did not make the world round or the Sabbath for man. The Lord says He made the Sabbath for man and made man "to dwell on all the face of the earth." The seventh day of the week which God has blessed comes to every nation on earth week by week. It is true that this day does not begin everywhere at the same time, but that does not in any sense prove that the same seventh day does not arrive to all people once every seven days.

Suppose there is a passenger ship making continuous trips around the world. We will say that it stops at every port on the circuit and takes on and discharges passengers. Suppose at every port some passengers get on and make the trip around the world and get off where they got on. Now they have all traveled on the same ship, but they did not all get on at the same time. Why didn't they? Simply because the world is round, and the ship could not arrive at every port at the same minute. But as it did arrive at port after port, the people got on; and so all rode on the same ship. So the Sabbath day travels around the world, and Sabbath observers living at all these ports are ready for it when it arrives; and as long as it remains with them, they observe it. So when the Sabbath has gone around the world, they all have observed the same day. When the Lord said, "The sabbath was made for man," and man was made to dwell on all the face of the earth, He knew whereof He was talking, and that He was not talking of an impossibility.

Is it a fact that if two men leave some seaport and travel around the world in opposite directions, one has actually gained twenty-four hours and the other lost the same number of hours? Such an arrangement is made simply to confuse those who do not think for themselves. One has not lived a minute longer or less than the other. (*See* Appendix.)

Suppose these two men were twin brothers, both born the same hour. Can we contend that when they left, they were exactly the same age and when they returned, one twin brother was forty-eight hours older than the other, and that thereafter they must celebrate their birthdays two days apart? Suppose they made one hundred trips; would you contend that one would be two hundred days older than the other? That would make, according to this theory, about seven months difference in their ages, although they were born the same hour. Every time they made the trip around the world, one would be twenty-four hours younger than he ought to be, and the other would be twenty-four hours older than he ought to be. The more one thinks of it, the more like nonsense it sounds.

People who observe God's holy Sabbath may be found all over the round world, and wherever they are, they are observing the day before the first day of the week as the Christians did in the New Testament times (Mark 16:1, 2). First-day observers have no trouble knowing when Sunday arrives anywhere on the globe.

There is one irrefutable geographical fact that forever disposes of the claim that the Sabbath cannot be kept on a round world because it comes to one place sooner than another, and that is this: The sun sets on one side of Palestine some minutes before it does on the other side. On one side of Palestine a man could be working during the closing minutes on the sixth day while on the other side a man could be resting on the opening minutes of the seventh day. This scripturally and geographically shatters the "can't keep Sabbath on a round world" argument. It is no more impossible to keep it on a round world than in Palestine, where the apostles lived and observed it.

The True Seventh Day

After all the man-invented arguments against the Sabbath of the Bible have been exploded by Scriptures of truth, some will ask, "How do you know which is the true seventh day?" That question is an admission that all the other arguments against the Sabbath are unsound, and that if it can be unquestionably proved that the day which we know as Saturday is the true seventh day on which the Creator rested, it is our Christian duty to keep it instead of some other day. In order to confuse the minds of the uninformed, Sunday advocates declare, "It has been some six thousand years since creation; we have no history covering many of those early centuries from creation to Moses; then how can we know today after thousands of years of tangled history during the rise and fall of kingdoms that there has been an accurate record of time kept since creation?

Of course to anyone who has never given the matter careful consideration, it will seem that the objector has won his point, and that it is an impossibility to locate the original seventh day. We are now ready to answer this question and give unanswerable proof that the day which we call Saturday is the original seventh day on which the Lord rested at the close of creation week thousands of years ago.

In the first place, let us say that we are not dependent upon man's memory or records for our knowledge of the Creator's rest day. The whole problem revolves around the question, Has the great God lost track of the day on which He rested? Suppose the people had lost the day between creation and Moses—does that prove that God had forgotten? Let us now see that the Lord never lost count of the days of the week between creation and Moses. When the Lord came down upon Sinai to proclaim the Ten Commandments, He said, "Remember the sabbath day to keep it holy."

Men were enjoined to remember the Creator's "rest" day. In the commandment He tells them to keep the day on which He, the Creator, rested because the rest day was the day He blessed. There were six days on which the Lord worked, and none of these could be His "rest" day. It is plain that to obey the Lord, men must necessarily rest the same day He rested at the close of creation week.

But how were they to know which day this was? We answer: Their knowledge of this matter did not depend upon man's wisdom but upon God's direct revelation. This revelation was made to them through the falling of the manna for forty years. "Six days ye shall gather it; but on the seventh day, which is the sabbath, in it there shall be none." Exodus 16:26.

In verse thirty-five of this chapter we read that the manna continued for "forty years." In a period of forty years there are more than two thousand weeks, and the Lord's rest day came once every week. On this day no manna fell. So certainly they knew at that time which was the true seventh day of the week. This sixteenth chapter of Exodus gives us Bible proof that God had not lost count of the day.

We next come to the time of the crucifixion, which was some fifteen hundred years later. Was the true seventh day known then? The Bible says it was. In Luke 23:56 we read that after placing the body of Jesus in the sepulcher, His followers "returned, and prepared spices and ointments; and rested the seventh day according to the commandment." Notice the words, "according to the commandment." There could be but one day that is the "sabbath day according to the commandment," because the commandment enjoins the observance of the identical day on which the Creator rested, and which He then blessed and sanctified. Apparently some four thousand years after creation the true Sabbath day had not been lost.

It has been some two thousand years since our Lord was crucified. How do we know that there has not been a day lost since that time? There are a number of irrefutable proofs that there has not, and that the day which we call Saturday is the same "sabbath day according to the commandment" on which the Christians rested after placing Jesus' body in Joseph's new tomb.

In the first place, none of the religious organizations deny that Saturday is the seventh day of the week. Ask the Baptists, the Methodists, or the Presbyterians whether they claim that the day which they are observing is the seventh day; and without an exception they will answer, "No, Sunday is the first day of the week."

All reference books, dictionaries, and encyclopedias declare that Saturday is the seventh day of the week. The calendars of all civilized nations, the world over, agree that Sunday is the first day of the week.

Astronomy Supports the Sabbath

Another irrefutable proof that there has not been a day lost is found in the science of astronomy, for astronomers could detect the slightest deviation in the weekly cycle. In *Sacred Chronology*, page 8, we read: "Go back three thousand years and stand upon the mighty watchtower in the temple of Belus, in old Babylon, and look out. The sun is sinking in eclipse, and great is the dismay of the terror-stricken inhabitants. We have the fact and circumstances recorded. But how shall we prove that the record is correct? The astronomer unravels the devious movements of the sun, the earth, and moon, through the whole period of three thousand years; with the power of intellect he goes back through the thirty long centuries, and announces that at such an hour, on such a day—as the Chaldean has written—that eclipse did take place."

So if there had been one hour lost during the past three thousand years, the science of astronomy could discover it.

A quotation on this point from the great astronomer Sir Isaac Newton will be of interest here.

The same thing I gather also thus. Cambyses began his reign in spring, *An*.J.P.(Year of the Julian Period) 4185 (B.C. 528), and reigned eight years, including the five months of Smerdes; and the [reign of] Darius Hystaspis began in spring, *An*.J.P.4193 (B.C. 520), and reigned thirty-six years, by the unanimous consent of all chronologers. The reigns of these two kings are determined by three eclipses of the moon observed in Babylon, and recorded by Ptolemy; so that it cannot be disputed. One was in the seventh year of Cambyses, *An*.J.P.4191 (B.C. 522), July 16, at 11 at night; another in the twentieth year of Darius, *An*.J.P.4212 (B.C. 501), November 19, at 11:45 at night; a third in the thirty-first year of Darius, *An*.J.P.4223 (B.C. 490), April 25, at 11:30 at night."—*Observations Upon the Prophecies of Daniel and the Apocalypse of St. John*, p. 233.

The more one thinks of it, the more it becomes evident that it is impossible to lose a day. The only way that the world could lose a day would be for all the world to retire on a certain night and sleep all that night, all the next day, the following night, and then all awaken at once after sleeping two nights and one day, thinking that they had slept only one night.

Calendar Change

Before leaving this part of the subject, I believe it will be well to give some attention to the change from the Julian calendar to the Gregorian. That change had absolutely nothing to do with the order of the days of the week. *The New International Encyclopedia* says, "It was ordained that ten days should be deducted from the year 1582, by calling what, according to the old calendar, would have been reckoned the 5th of October, the 15th of October, 1582."

That was all that was done. They called the fifth of October the fifteenth. Both days were Thursdays. The next day was Friday just the same. The only difference was that it was the sixteenth of the month instead of the sixth. The Greek Catholic Church did not adopt this change until 1923, but when it was Saturday in Greece, it was Saturday in every other European country, although a different date of the month.

Another proof that there has not been a day lost and that the day we call Saturday is the seventh day of the week is the fact that the ancient nations, in naming over the days of the week, call the day which we in English know as Saturday by the sacred name "Sabbath." I once addressed a question to The Institute of International Information in association with *Our World* magazine, inquiring whether the Greek word designating the day which we call in English Saturday is equivalent to our word "Sabbath." I also asked which nations call Saturday Sabbath when naming the days of the week. The answers received to these two questions are as follows:

"The Greek *sabbaton* is the rendering from the old Hebrew *shabbath* of which our word 'Sabbath' is a later form. The French, Italian, Spanish, Portuguese, and German words for Saturday are all derived from this root also."

In the face of all the evidence here given, who can with the least degree of authority and proof contend that Saturday is not the seventh day of the week hallowed by the Creator at the close of creation week? There is no man living who would be foolish enough even to attempt to refute this evidence.

Sabbath Worship

A man connected with a certain Bible institute says: "The Sabbath law required them [the Israelites] to remain at home. How would this affect church attendance?" This writer quotes Exodus 16, beginning with verse twenty-six:

"Six days ye shall gather it; but on the seventh day, which is the sabbath, in it there shall be none. And it came to pass, that there went out some of the people on the seventh day for to gather, and they found none. And the Lord said unto Moses, How long refuse ye to keep my commandments and my laws? See, for that the Lord hath given you the sabbath, therefore he giveth you on the sixth day the bread of two days; abide ye every man in his place, let no man go out of his place on the seventh day. So the people rested on the seventh day."

What the Lord meant was that no man should "go out of his place" to gather manna on the seventh day. That He did not mean that the Israelites were not to leave their dwellings to attend divine service on the Sabbath ought to be known by anyone who has the least knowledge of the Scriptures. In fact, God's people were instructed to attend public worship on the Sabbath: "Six days shall work be done: but the seventh day is the sabbath of rest, an holy convocation; ye shall do no work therein: it is the sabbath of the Lord in all your dwellings." Leviticus 23:3.

The Sabbath was to be a day of "holy convocation." All informed people know that the word "convocation" means "a publicly assembled congregation." (See any dictionary.) David said, "I went with them to the house of God, with the voice of joy and praise, with a multitude that kept holyday." Psalm 42:4. Here we find that multitudes went "to the house of God" on the Sabbath day. Certainly they had to leave their places of abode to go to the house of God.

Then coming to the times of Jesus, we find that "as his custom was, he went into the synagogue on the sabbath day, and stood up for to read" (Luke 4:16). Certainly during the years when He was being "brought up," it was necessary, as He went to the place of worship on the Sabbath, to leave His humble home with Joseph and Mary. Then, too, "Jesus went on the sabbath day through the corn." Matthew 12:1. He had to leave His place of residence to do that. We read in Luke's account, in Acts 16:13, of the stay in Philippi: "And on the sabbath we went out of the city by a river side, where prayer was wont to be made." In face of all these texts, how can any man claim that those who observed the Sabbath were required to remain shut up in their homes all day? The Scriptures teach that one purpose of the Sabbath was to give opportunity for all to come "together to hear the word of God" (Acts 13:44).

The Sabbath Is Above the Ceremonial Law

It has been pointed out by opponents of the Sabbath that the Israelites in the wilderness were not to kindle a fire on the Sabbath day. These same Sabbath haters claim that in the wintertime the children of Israel suffered by being cold all the day. The claim is certainly far from the truth. For one thing, they were in a very hot region; hence the only reason for a fire would be for working, which they were told to do on Friday. Why will men picture God as being merciless and without pity just to provide themselves with a specious argument against an unwelcome truth? How far from the truth this is, is discovered by the Lord's own command to "call the sabbath a delight" (Isaiah 58:13). The dictionary defines "delight" as "that which affords joyful satisfaction."

Speaking of the showbread, the Lord gave this instruction: "Every sabbath he shall set it in order before the Lord continually." Leviticus 24:8. Jesus said, "I am that bread of life." The showbread represented Christ, "the bread of life." The renewing of this bread every Sabbath simply meant that the Sabbath is a day for the renewal of spiritual life, and it is to be spent in going "to hear the word of God" (Acts 13:44), in going "to the house of God, with the voice of joy and praise." Because of this privilege we are to call the Sabbath a delight.

The fourth commandment has probably contributed more to the spiritual life of man than any other of the ten. Is this why the devil hates it? Does this explain why the devil has always encouraged Sabbath desecration? Is it not natural that the devil should seek to destroy the Sabbath in order that man may be deprived of its spiritual advantages? This being the case, long should remain silent the tongue of puny man before raising his voice against it by arguments which are as far from the truth as anything could possibly be.

Whatever circumstances made it unnecessary to "kindle" a fire, one can be sure God's instruction never detracted one whit from the command, "Call the sabbath a delight, the holy of the Lord, honourable; and . . . honor him, not doing thine own ways, nor finding thine own pleasure, nor speaking thine own words," or from the promise, "Then shalt thou delight thyself in the Lord" (Isaiah 58:13, 14). In the crude ways of kindling a fire even two centuries ago, men had to work exhaustively with flint and tinder to get it started. Fires were kept from going out because it was so difficult to kindle a new one. Perhaps this explains God's command.

Chapter 12

Bible Answers

Before closing this book, I wish to suggest a number of questions and offer Bible answers which I believe will fortify and verify every conclusion reached in the foregoing pages. These questions are as follows:

1. Who made the Sabbath?
2. When was the Sabbath made?
3. How was the Sabbath made?
4. For whom was the Sabbath made?
5. Out of what was the Sabbath made?
6. For what purpose was the Sabbath made?
7. For how long a time was the Sabbath made?

Taking up these propositions in their order, I offer the following Bible answers:

Who made the Sabbath? In the first place, it is scriptural to say that the Sabbath was "made," for Jesus said, "The sabbath was made for man." Now who made the Sabbath? Everything that is made must have a maker. It was Jesus who made the Sabbath, for speaking of Him, John says, "He was in the world, and the world was made by him." John 1:10. Then in verse three we read, "All things were made by him; and without him was not any thing made that was made." Then if the Sabbath was "made," if Christ made "all things," if "without him was not any thing made that was made"—well, I leave it to you whether the Bible teaches that Christ made the Sabbath. Then, too, that which pertains to Christ is "Christian"; therefore the seventh day is the Christian Sabbath. There could be no conclusion that is more normal, more natural, or more scriptural. This is why we have contended in this book that the Lord's day is the Sabbath—it was the Lord who made it.

When was the Sabbath made? The Bible says it was made at the close of creation week, nearly twenty-five hundred years before Sinai or the Jews.

"Thus the heavens and the earth were finished, and all the host of them. And on the seventh day God ended [ceased] his work which he had made; and he rested on the seventh day from all his work which he had made. And God blessed the seventh day, and sanctified it: because that in it he had rested from all his work which God created and made." Genesis 2:1–3.

In speaking of this later, God said, "Wherefore the Lord blessed the sabbath day." This proves that from the beginning the seventh day was called the sabbath day. So the Sabbath was made in Eden before man sinned, not twenty-five hundred years later at Sinai. No one who believes the Bible will deny this.

How was the Sabbath made? Only the Creator could make the Sabbath because only the Creator can create a world. Neither the popes nor the disciples could make a Sabbath day, for they cannot create. God did four things when He made the Sabbath. First, he rested after creating the world. Second, He blessed the Sabbath day. Third, He sanctified it. Fourth, He hallowed the Sabbath day. This shows how impossible it would be for man to change or make a Sabbath. The fact that the Creator "rested" on, "blessed," "sanctified," and "hallowed" the Sabbath day shows how very sacred is this institution. It makes understandable why the Lord wants us to keep it holy.

For whom was the Sabbath made? It doesn't take long to answer that question. Jesus forever settled it when He said, "The sabbath was made for man." Mark 2:27. The word "man" in this text is *anthropos* (Greek) and means "all mankind, irrespective of nationality or sex." It is the same word that is translated "man" in John 1:9, which refers to "every man that cometh into the world." It is scripturally sure that it is not "the Jewish Sabbath" but "the sabbath of the Lord thy God" that was made for "every man that cometh into the world."

Out of what was the Sabbath made? The Sabbath was made out of the particular day of the week on which the Creator rested: "He rested the seventh day." It was made out of the day which the Creator blessed: "God blessed the seventh day." It was made out of the day which the Creator separated from the other six working days and sanctified: God "sanctified" the seventh day. The only way for any other day to be the Sabbath day would be for this resting, blessing, sanctifying, and hallowing to be stripped from the seventh day and transferred to it. And this could not be done, for the Creator never rested any other day. Luke 23:56 says, "They . . . rested the sabbath day according to the commandment," and this was the day before the first day of the week. If the day after Jesus died, Saturday, the seventh day, is "the sabbath day according to the commandment," then it is scripturally incorrect to apply the wording of the fourth commandment to the first day of the week or to any day other than the one on which the Creator rested. This overthrows the argument that "just any day will do."

For what purpose was the Sabbath made? The Scriptures give several reasons. These reasons are just as fundamental and eternal today as at any other time in the history of the world. The reason assigned in the Sabbath commandment is comprehended in the words, "For in six days the *Lord* made heaven and earth." Its observance stands for the observer's belief that God—not some unknown power—is the Creator. In view of the theory of evolution, so rampant in the educational institutions of all the world today, surely the weekly reminder of God's creatorship is important. Next, the Sabbath was made to be a day of physical rest and a day of worship. "The seventh day is . . . an holy convocation." "Convocation" means "an assembly of any sort." But the Sabbath is set apart as a day of "holy" convocation, a convocation exclusively for holy purposes. It is a day for assembling for worship. David said, "I went with them to the house of God, with the voice of joy and praise, with a multitude that kept holyday." Psalm 42:4. It was the same in the New Testament in apostolic times. "The next sabbath day came almost the whole city together to hear the word of God." Acts 13:44. Please keep in mind we are getting a Bible answer to the question, For what purpose was the Sabbath made? In the Old Testament we found, "I went with them to the house of God . . . with a multitude that kept holyday." Just so in the New Testament. Such worship was to be a safeguard against idolatry and against evolution (denying God as the Creator). It was to be a blessing to man physically, as well as spiritually.

For how long a time was the Sabbath made? The only answer is this: As long as man needs that for which it provides. As long as man needs rest from physical labor of six days, as long as it is necessary for man to recognize God as the Creator of the world, as long as it is important that mankind should come together to hear the Word of God, the Sabbath will last. Thus the Sabbath will last not only till the end of this world, but to all eternity.

When the original beauty of the earth is restored and every trace of sin eliminated; when man is changed from mortality to immortality, and is again formed in the image and likeness of his Creator and Redeemer, the Sabbath will never again be desecrated. "For as the new heavens and the new earth, which I will make, shall remain before me, saith the Lord, so shall your seed and your name remain. And it shall come to pass, that from one new moon to another, and from one sabbath to another, shall all flesh come to worship before me, saith the Lord." Isaiah 66:22, 23. It is my prayer that you may be in that glorious new earth.

Appendix

The Sabbath on a Round World

It is well for Sabbathkeepers to be cognizant of certain intellectual challenges which face us today; these include deciding how to keep Sabbath in an age of jet travel, of scientific stations in Antarctica and of a proposed new calendar for the European Union.

The rotation of the earth under the sun accounts for sunset, and the time of sunset (relative to noon) at a particular place depends on both latitude and terrain. A sedentary Sabbathkeeper has no problem with these variations, for he can see sunset and make his decision regarding the hours of Sabbath on that observation. But a person who travels around the world and returns to his original location, if he is traveling eastward, experiences somewhat shorter days (or if westward, longer days) than the one who stays home. These time differences add up to one sunset gained or lost in going around the world. This is a geometric, mathematical fact, and seems to a non-Sabbathkeeping skeptic an insoluble problem

Let us say that the round-the-world trip takes about a week, and the Sabbathkeeper keeps Sabbath by local sundown wherever he finds himself during that week. Then when he arrives back home he finds that his count of sundowns differs from his neighbor's by one, so that if he continues his traveling count he is faced with two Sabbaths, and which to choose? The devout Sabbathkeeper will not find difficulty in keeping both days in the first week at home—he needs the rest anyway.

The dweller in the land of the midnight sun, where sunsets may cease for months, must regulate his Sabbathkeeping otherwise: by position of sun or stars, by clock, or by electronic communication with other parts of the world.

The would-be astronaut must choose between his fidelity to the commandment and his desire to be involved in worldly pursuits on Sabbath.

The proposed new calendar poses a different kind of problem, for it is intended to include leap-days every month, upsetting the 7-day cycle so that Sabbath comes on a different day of the week from month to month. Is this aimed at Sabbathkeepers, to make it difficult specifically for them to maintain employment? The true Sabbathkeeper in such a situation would need to maintain a separate calendar to regulate his spiritual life.

–Editor

Scripture Index

Subject Index